9/25/05

To Taylor

Our Very Best to U

God Bless Kay g

Ronda Hyman

&

Rick Hyman

My Texas Family
An Uncommon Journey to Prosperity

Featuring photographs from 1912 to 1927

From left to right are Ellen Martin Johnson, Etnar Ligon, and Cornelius Martin. Ellen and Cornelius were sisters; Etnar was their cousin. Ellen was Rick Hyman's grandmother.

MY TEXAS FAMILY
An Uncommon Journey to Prosperity

Featuring photographs from 1912 to 1927

Rick Hyman and Ronda Hyman

Rick Hyman

Ronda Hyman

EsoWon Books

TEMPUS

Published by Arcadia Publishing,
An imprint of Tempus Publishing, Inc.
2 Cumberland Street
Charleston, SC 29401

Printed in Great Britain.

Library of Congress Catalog Card Number: 98-86142

For general information contact Tempus Publishing at:
Telephone 843-853-2070
Fax 843-853-0044
E-Mail sales@arcadiapublishing.com

For customer service and orders:
Toll-Free 1-888-313-2665

Visit us on the internet at http://www.arcadiaimages.com

CONTENTS

About the
Authors

Rick and Ronda Hyman

Gifted from birth, Rick Hyman has been painting since he was three years old. His vibrant and compelling works have been appreciated by millions, including Bill Cosby, who has a print of *My Texas Family* on the set of *Cosby*. This painting, featured on the cover of the book, was the first of Hyman's acclaimed series of historical family portraits.

Inspired by a treasured collection of family photographs and conversations with elderly relatives, Hyman is preserving his heritage through his acrylic paintings. His work has been exhibited at the Salmagundi Club on New York's Fifth Avenue, Union Station in Washington, D.C., the Institute of Texan Cultures in San Antonio, the Daura Gallery at Lynchburg College in Lynchburg, Virginia, and the Nevada Arts Council Gallery in Las Vegas, Nevada. A three-year traveling exhibition of Hyman's family portrait series, sponsored by the Virginia Museum of Fine Arts, began touring museums across the country in October 1999.

Rick Hyman consults with his wife, Ronda, on all of his artwork and hopes to paint all 300 photographs in his lifetime.

Ronda Cain Hyman was born and raised in Nashville, Tennessee. She attended St. Vincent de Paul Elementary School and Cathedral High School, an all-girls private school in Nashville. Ronda enjoyed a short singing career right after high school. She is a writer and poet and studied psychology at the University of Tennessee and multicultural diversity at The American University in Washington, D.C., where she met her husband, Rick.

When the couple met (and married) in 1993, they were overwhelmed when they found that their values, goals, dreams, and the importance they placed on family were almost identical. Rick was further along than Ronda in documenting his family history, which he had begun in 1980. Ronda joined Rick in the project by traveling with him to Texas and other states to gather information from family members and other sources.

The Hymans currently reside in Las Vegas, Nevada, and can be reached by email at the following address: hymanart@aol.com.

ACKNOWLEDGMENTS

Rick: I would like to thank my father and mother, the late Bruce L. Hyman Sr. and the late Ida Mae Johnson Hyman, for their love and encouragement of my talents, especially in art, which they saw at an early age. My aunt, the late Gussie Lee Johnson, for holding on to the photographs and other memorabilia over the years. My uncle, the late Dr. Mark Hyman, historian, author, and mentor, for suggesting that I paint these vintage photographs. My stepmother, Marguerite Butler, who believed in me and still does. My brother, Bruce Hyman Jr., and his wife, Denise, and their daughter, Shenise, and my nephews, Darryl and Guy Marshall, for all of their love and support.

Thank you to Earl Hunt, a lifelong friend. Charles Young Elementary School in Washington, D.C., for recognizing my artistic abilities and allowing me to use my imagination freely. Special thanks to Thomas (Skip) Johnson, who was like another older brother to me while growing up in Northeast Washington, D.C., and to his mother, Helen Johnson, who was like family to us. Carlean Stanley and her son (my godson) Louis Stanley Jr., for all of their encouragement and support, especially at the beginning of my career.

Great appreciation goes to my cousins, the late Bernice McLaughlin and Mamie Paige White, who spent time with us sharing our rich family history and identifying some of the people in the photographs. My cousins, Everett and Eliza Martin Calhoun, for also helping to identify some of the family members in the photographs. Evelyn McLaughlin (wife of the late Bernice McLaughlin), Raymond Martin Sr., Willie Martin, and R.B. and Marjorie Martin Tones for telling me about my Texas family on my grandmother's side (Ellen Martin Johnson of La Grange and Houston, Texas). Ms. Helen Debato Stewart (my mother's best friend growing up), who shared information and encouraged me with this book.

Thank you to James and Jerlean Williams, Clarence and Cleo McIntosh, Rev. Willie Williams, Leonard and Minnie Mann, Grace Williams, Cleo and Dorothy Metcalf, Tommy and Mollie Thorne, James and Vickie Franklin, who are family on my grandfather's side (Ell Johnson of La Grange and Houston), for simply being loving and dedicated family members, supporting this book project, and constantly reinforcing the importance of family reunions.

Ronda: I thank my mother, the late Helen Marine Cain, and my father, R.B. Joseph Cain, for always loving and encouraging me and Rick, not only throughout this project, but on a daily basis as well. My brother Randall and my sisters Dona, Terris,

Joy, and Monica, whose closeness, love, and humor helped keep me in good spirits, especially during the time of learning to live without our mother. Ms. Mary Brown (Nan, my mother's godmother), who has nothing but praises and good wishes for us.

Thanks to Nina Graybill for leading us in the right direction. Deborah Parker for opening her home to us many times during the early stages of this book. Linda Wolfe Keister, who profoundly supports our art and this family history project. Our best friends, Terry and Sheila Elliott and Bob and Alice Ammons, for all their love and support over the years. Janice Magona and Pat Gibson for falling in love with the artwork and making it possible for it to be displayed at the historical landmark, Union Station in Washington, D.C. Stevens Carter, artist, for being instrumental in exposing Rick's art in Washington, D.C.

Thank you to Beverly Hyman Reynolds, Rick's first cousin, who is always there to help us in any way she can. Johnny Johnson, artist, art professor, and mentor, who was one of the first to recognize Rick's unique style of painting. Rafi Shahidi, who predicted his future in art. Martha Hamilton, who was the first one to encourage us to write a book.

Many thanks for celebrating our art and family history project through exhibitions go to Eileen Mott of the Virginia Museum of Fine Arts, Virginia Davis of the Daura Gallery at Lynchburg College in Virginia, and Leah Lewis, Dr. Shirley Mock, and Dr. Barbara Lawrence of the University of Texas Institute of Texan Cultures in San Antonio.

Thanks go to the Fayette Heritage Museum and Archives and the Fayette Public Library for assisting with research on La Grange, Warrenton, and Round Top, Texas.

We wish to thank Allison Carpenter, our Acquisitions Editor at Arcadia Publishing, for her vision and special dedication to this book project and for being so wonderful to work with. We appreciate Lou Stovall of the District of Columbia Commission on the Arts and Humanities, for putting many hours of thought and research into my artwork in writing the foreword for this book. Many thanks to Sheree Scarborough of the University of Texas Center for American History for her contribution in writing a foreword for this book, for her research on Texas history, and for her appreciation of our family's legacy.

We especially thank our daughters, Christy Hardison Bean, Brianna Hardison, and Ellen Merissa Hyman, for their endless love and support, as well as Adam Crouch, who is like family to us and whose love and support we truly appreciate; Christy's husband, our son-in-law, James Bean, who we couldn't be more proud of; and James and Christy's new baby girl, Soler Brazille Bean, born September 16, 1999, who we welcome to the family tree as our first grandchild.

The information in this book is believed to be as accurate as possible. We gathered information from relatives, family friends, and other sources as best we could.

AGAINST ALL ODDS:
Rick Hyman's Remarkable Texas Family

by Sheree Scarborough, The University of Texas at Austin

African-American historian Rayford W. Logan has referred to the late 19th and early 20th century in America as the "nadir of the Negro." This lowest point came at the end of Reconstruction in the South, where 90 percent of the African-American population continued to live at the turn of the century, and the simultaneous abandonment of black rights by many Northern whites. It was a time of Jim Crow laws that segregated public facilities, provided for unequal education, disenfranchisement, and racial violence. In fact, after a series of race riots, the National Association for the Advancement of Colored People (NAACP) was founded in New York in 1910, in order to avert a "race war." It is into this unlikely set of historical circumstances that we find Rick Hyman's ancestors flourishing in Fayette County, Texas.

The story of Hyman's ancestors—the Martins, Robersons, Ligons, Alexanders, Dobbins, and Walkers—in some ways tells the larger story of African Americans after the Civil War and into the next century, and in other ways is uniquely their own. The wagon train that made its way from Virginia to Texas toward the end of the war was part of a larger migration of ex-slaves out of the South, which took place in the years following the war. During the late 1860s and 1870s, many

These students are posing in the 1920s or 30s in front of the wooden Randolph High School in La Grange. The teacher was Mr. G.A. Randolph. This school went from first grade all the way up to the tenth. After completing the tenth grade, the kids were ready to go to college.

African Americans moved to the farmlands of Oklahoma, Louisiana, and Texas. The rich farmland found in Fayette County was a likely place to settle. Located in south central Texas, Fayette County is part of the Blackland Prairies region of the state and is a pathway for the Colorado River; thus, it has an abundance of fertile soil, water, and wildlife. It was part of Stephen F. Austin's first Texas colony in the 1820s, but settlement predated even that with Native-American inhabitants and European and Mexican settlers. It suffices to say that Fayette County is a rich agricultural region that has always lured settlers.

As was true across the South, the post–Civil War era was a time of change and upheaval in Fayette County. The war had wreaked economic hardship on the predominantly German and Slav community of farmers and planters. However, from 1870 to the turn of the century, Fayette County experienced a period of growth. Newcomers to the county at this time included a large influx of mainly Germans, Czechs, Bohemians, and Wends. The number of small farms and areas under cultivation increased dramatically. For the African-American population, of course, the shift following the Civil War was profound; it was the shift from slavery to freedom. Economically, however, it was a difficult period that only brought slight improvement. Most of the county's African-American population became sharecroppers and received only one-third of the crop they farmed in payment. Even so—and despite the increasing numbers of white immigrants—the county's African-American population continued to grow. In 1870 it was one-fifth the total population and in 1900 it had grown to one-third.

Although the African-American population in Fayette County grew stronger in numbers during this period, it was an extremely difficult time in all other ways for them. It was the nadir. Reconstruction in Texas, immediately following the Civil War, was a time marked by restrictions of freedom and violence against African Americans. Black Codes were enacted by the state legislature to restrict African-Americans' newly won freedoms and, worse, there was a wave of violence of white against black. The violence prompted the U.S. Congress to send the military to Texas and institute a period of military rule. The Black Codes were dropped and

Fayette County is located in central Texas, near Austin.

violence against African Americans diminished, but it did not stop. Lynching continued in Texas through the 1940s and, in fact, was a dominant theme playing out on the landscape while Henderson Martin was establishing himself and his family. The 1893 lynching of Henry Smith in Paris, Texas, was one of the first blatantly public lynchings in the South. Twenty-three years later, in 1916, Jesse Washington was lynched in the City Hall square in Waco, only 150 miles from Fayette County.

The first two decades of the 20th century continued to be a time of economic, legal, and political hardship for most African Americans in Texas. The poll tax was established in 1903, the white primary in 1906, and there was segregation of public transportation, accommodations, and, of course, education. Most African Americans in Texas continued to farm, but only 20 percent owned their own land. Most farmed land as tenants. African Americans were second-class citizens who were denied the basic rights of citizenship. However, the story found in the photographs of this book, the story of African-American industry, intelligence, perseverance, and joy, is a story that runs throughout the course of African-American history in this country. Against all odds, African Americans defended themselves and their families. They established churches, schools, and colleges; built communities based on self-help, economic development, and mutual values; created thriving businesses such as grocery stores, funeral homes, newspapers, and photography studios; and continued to farm the land.

At a time when most African Americans in Fayette County, or for that matter the nation, were struggling for survival, Henderson Martin and his family had established themselves as landowners and joined the ranks of the middle-class. This remarkable African-American Texas family owned oil-rich land, bought carriages, automobiles, and jewelry, educated its children, and incredibly, for us, documented itself. Rick Hyman's great aunt Cornelius Martin picked up the camera and recorded the daily life of her exceptional experience. The photographs show a proud and friendly family who pose with their possessions, not unlike photographs we have from white middle-class families from the same time period, which would later become part of the middle-class fabric of both black and white families, both casual and studio photography.

This cache of photographs is important to our understanding of a particular time in history, for a certain group of people. It sheds light on the daily life and activities of middle-class African Americans in Fayette County, Texas—a story that happened very rarely and is documented even more rarely—in the first two decades of the 20th century. But it tells us much more than that. These photographs stand as a testament to the strength of spirit that enabled a family to emerge from slavery, survive a trying time filled with physical dangers and restrictions in every part of their lives, and prosper in an atmosphere of segregation and second-class citizenship. Indeed, they stand as a testament to the strength of spirit for all of us. At the very lowest point—beyond slavery—for African Americans in America, Rick Hyman's family arrived in Texas, prospered, and passed on the legacy to the next generation, the generation after that, and to all who find this story meaningful.

Fayette County Courthouse, c. 1920.

SOURCES

Barr, Alwyn. *Black Texans: A History of African Americans in Texas, 1528–1995.* University of Oklahoma Press, 1996.

Davis, George A. and O. Fred Donaldson, eds. *Blacks in the United States: A Geographic Perspective.* Boston: Houghton Mifflin Company, 1975.

Govenar, Alan. *Portraits of Community: African American Photography in Texas.* Austin: Texas State Historical Association, 1996.

Hale, Grace Elizabeth. *Making Whiteness: The Culture of Segregation in the South, 1890–1940.* New York: Pantheon Books, 1998.

Hickman, R.C. *Behold the People: R.C. Hickman's Photographs of Black Dallas, 1949–1961.* Austin: Texas State Historical Association, 1994.

Lewis, David Levering. *W.E.B. DuBois: Biography Of A Race.* New York: Henry Holt And Company, 1993.

Logan, Rayford W. *The Negro in the United States, Volume I: A History to 1945—From Slavery to Second-class Citizenship.* Van Nostrand Reinhold Company, 1970.

Williams, David A. *Bricks Without Straw: A Comprehensive History of African Americans in Texas.* Austin: Eakin Press, 1997.

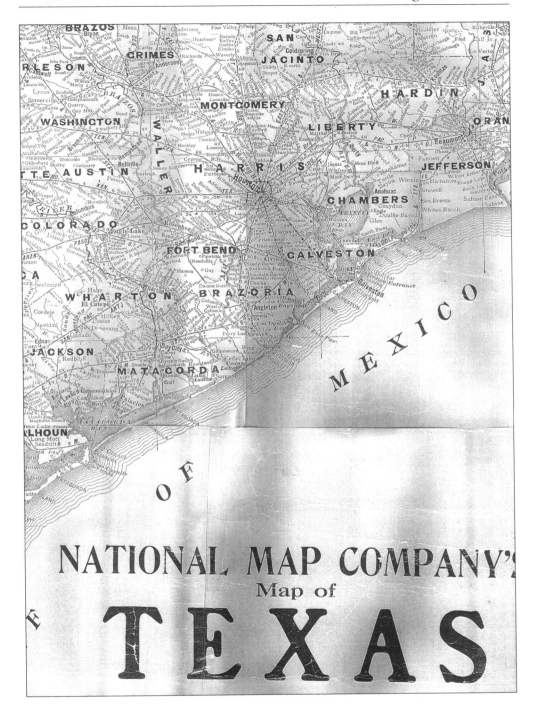

This map of south Texas shows Fayette County in the top left-hand corner.

MAKING OUR WAY TO SOMETHING BETTER:

An Understanding of Rick Hyman's Narrative Paintings

by Lou Stovall, Vice Chairman of the D.C. Commission on the Arts and Humanities

Rick Hyman's paintings are arresting. His straightforward, innocent style captures your interest and invites you to know his subjects. His subjects are familiar, friendly people with clear eyes that are engaging. Set in landscapes and in front of the occasional building, these rural narratives are personal—Hyman's own history—as you will learn quickly upon speaking with him. Hyman characterizes his work as <u>historical paintings</u>, but that gives us insight only to the source of the inspiration. As with almost every storyteller, motivation is the stronger imperative. Hyman has realized his desire to make pictures from the age of three. He was a diligent student in school and at home. His mother, a teacher, made decorating the school bulletin board an art, and Hyman remembers that his first significant responses to color came at his mother's side. He continued to be fascinated with art through high school and later took a few classes in painting and art history while attending American University in Washington, D.C. After college, he became a self-styled, self-motivated student of the arts by reading extensively and visiting museums.

By 1981, when he came upon a cache of vintage photographs in the home of a relative, he was ready to be an artist; a door opened for him, and his true calling was ignited. He grasped the opportunity much the same as his great-grandfather had grasped his opportunity years before. Henderson Martin was a free man, born in Texas in 1866. During his youth, he worked on the ranch of Martin Liggons (a white man), a cattle rancher with large holdings of land. Sometime around the 1880s, Henderson Martin purchased 70 acres of land from the Longler family. He arranged to pay $25 per month, thereby becoming a businessman and cattle rancher at an early age. He had learned to read, write, and do arithmetic as a child from Martin Liggons, who was a significant and positive presence in the life of Henderson. Before his death, he gave 2,000 acres of land to Henderson.

Rick Hyman painted Making Our Way to Something Better *to illustrate his family's covered wagon journey around 1864. Please turn to p. 122 for a color representation and more information about this painting.*

Henderson was the son of Cezar Martin, a slave on the plantation of the Roberson family. Cezar gained his freedom sometime around 1863. He migrated from that Virginia plantation with four covered wagons, arriving in Texas in February of 1864. During the long journey west, relationships with Native Americans occurred often. Friendships and marriages were made. As Hyman understands the history of his ancestors, his great-great-grandfather, Cezar Martin, was a good man who had meaningful dealings with his Native-American relatives. Henderson Martin continued the relationship and was told, among other things, that there was oil underground on his land. While taking a walk along the creek one day, Henderson's heel ruptured the shallow bank of the creek and the water suddenly turned black. Henderson Martin had struck oil. Blessed with opportunity, Henderson Martin did not waste his good fortune. He taught his family well.

Like his fathers before him, Rick Hyman was raised to make the best of himself. He thought himself blessed with the discovery of the photographs.

It was a visual substantiation of his family's history. He began to ask more questions, seeking to make connections between the stories and the tales. With the encouragement of family and friends, he summoned up his strengths.

Hyman had become the keeper of the family flame, and in 1996 he became their narrator. The art of the narrative is an epiphany. It is the blessing that keeps us close to our ancestors, close to our land, and ultimately, close to ourselves. Hyman is a good and generous man. His spirit and his paintings reflect his concern for other people. He is quiet-spoken, gentle, and welcoming. He shares his connection to the land. His work is about that connection. It is a meaningful, symbolic gesture that his subjects stand squarely on rich red-brown soil. Conversely, our positive reaction to Hyman's paintings is not accidental. His paintings are about us, as well as the land, and they appeal to the broad cross-section of our national quilt. In this busy world of ours, it is rare to find easy-to-love art that is unabashedly sentimental, informative, and likable.

When I first met Rick Hyman, he was effusive, and I was caught up in his excitement as he told the story of his Texas family. From those beautiful old photographs, he began to paint the legacy of his family. Hyman, an adventurous colorist, makes choices and combinations suggested by his imagination and the colors in a trove of beautiful jewelry discovered with the photographs. Family members added their recollections of style and color. We can sense the feel of the leather sling hood and the maroon velvet-covered seats of the Model-T Ford, a proud family car painted clean and shiny black, evidence of his ancestors' good fortune. The red dirt, baked by the sun, is hard and hot underfoot. The grass is lush and just a little cool around the ankles. No bare feet here—his forebearers are dressed in their Sunday finery. The dresses are of silk and good cotton, and the boys' pants seem to be velvet. The suits are well cut, and the hats are Stetsons. Typical of the period's financial stability, Sunday afternoons were for picture taking.

Hyman paints naturally. Essentially, Hyman paints what he sees. When a sense of space is needed, he relies upon basic tools of perspective to establish a horizon line and vanishing point, as in *Family Tree*. The configuration of the hills in the background exaggerates the vanishing point. All eyes are outlined and focused toward the frontal plane, and the table and the branches of the tree seem to recede and establish standing room for the family members. Perhaps from observations of the work of early Abstract Expressionist painters, he uses deep reds and varied browns to make the building on the left seem to move forward, as the yellow tablecloth is pulled back in response to the green of the lawn, the hills, and the foliage. He has used color and structure to make his point. Hyman may be presupposing the longevity of his family tree in choosing to emphasize the depth of field in the painting through structure and through color.

Hyman is aware of the rules of picture painting. His subjects are up front, mostly in the foreground. In *Women in the Field*, the grass and the trees are rhythmically arranged and painted much the same as the brush strokes of the late Impressionists. Hyman paints full-figured representations of his subjects.

Historical artist Rick Hyman, in his element with paintbrush and pallet, in Vienna, Virginia, April 1999.

Rick Hyman's great aunts, Mabel, Alice, and Nora, in La Grange. These women appear in the painting From These Beginnings, *which appears at the end of this book.*

His use of foreshortening tends to bring his subjects closer to the frontal plane, creating a different kind of tension than of the threesome by the Model-T Ford in *My Texas Family*. The rendering of clothing with medium to short diagonal strokes throughout his painting is an Expressionist technique that set the standard for a quick capture of subject.

The application of paint on canvas is informed, reminiscent of established styles. In *Undefeated*, Hyman embraces architectural realism. The treatment of stone, brick, and mortar is accurate. In this same painting, he uses his unique approach to render the clothing in both realistic and abstract manners. Hyman's brush strokes vary from heavy stippling and short, choppy dabs to long pulls; a combination of Impressionist and Expressionist technique.

With a brief switch from technical considerations of Hyman's work, I find the painting *My Texas Family* utterly charming. The family is rendered as a quick sketch, while the Model-T Ford is painstakingly detailed. He understands the beauty of dappled things and paints foliage accordingly. And the most beautiful part of all is his treatment of the tree on the left. With trees generally heavily shaded in order to establish space, Hyman's treatment of the foliage seems to reach back stylistically to late Italian Renaissance paintings.

Southern Gentlemen on a Sunday Afternoon may well sum up Hyman's perception of his family as genteel, education-seeking, and hard-working.

Hyman's treatment of eyes is consistent, but an added feature is that we seem to have a familiarity with these men, as if we could get to know them—or have known them.

From the stories told about his ancestors, Hyman visualized the wagon train formed by his great-great-grandfather, Cezar Martin. In *Making Our Way to Something Better*, Cezar is painted with a large hat and horizontally striped pants (presumably made from mattress ticking). His wife is beside him and the three other women appear in long dresses with bonnets and aprons typical of the times. Each of the four wagons is pulled by two mules. The diminutive, rolling hills in the background are more like the hills of Anacostia near the northeast area of Washington, D.C., where Hyman grew up. It is easy to imagine the hills and the open sky of Hyman's positive childhood experiences transferred to the imagined landscape of his ancestors' move west. Definite maturing of Hyman's handling of the people and the mules is evident in this painting. The lead wagon seems to be actually moving, as do the four walking figures. It is interesting that the trees are not represented as major elements of the composition. The brush strokes, while more abstract, result in a more realistic representation.

In *Making Our Way to Something Better*, Hyman has realistically represented the upgraded style and furnishings of his subjects. Notice the sophisticated hair treatment, the stylish hats, and the beautiful dresses. And, like their male counterparts in *Southern Gentlemen*, the women in *Making Our Way to Something Better* represent a generation established and at ease in a new prosperity. When looking at Hyman's paintings individually, we see facial features that we recognize from previous paintings. Making these connections is enjoyable.

By using the black-and-white and sepia-toned photographs as a starting point, Hyman's rendering of these subjects in color introduces a new way of looking at some interesting details of an undiscovered past. In each successive painting, his ability to render facial expressions, clothing, and surroundings improves. He continues to learn and to grow as an artist.

When Hyman refers to his direct history using the stories that he has gained from older relatives, he remembers the stories of the ranch. He notes that no photograph was found of anyone actually riding on a horse. In *My Horse, My Carriage, My Land*, Hyman's great-great-grandfather, George P. Ligon (Henderson Martin's wife's father), is as tall as the horse. His arm is draped over the horse in a caring manner. With a rancher, the horse is well-represented as a best friend.

Hyman has an extraordinary grasp of his subjects' lives and personalities, and he brings forth a sense of history and narrative that goes beyond the photographs. We see emotion here—a sense of caring and pride. He is giving us a fresh breath of the past.

INTRODUCTION

by Ronda Hyman

In every family there is a chosen one—one who is the keeper of the family heirlooms, the photo album, and the collector of stories. In this family, a camera fell into a great-aunt's hands (Cornelius Martin), and a paintbrush fell into a great-grandson's hands (Rick Hyman). Hyman's Aunt Cornelius was a master at capturing a lifetime of tradition and family history on film. Now, Rick Hyman is celebrating and keeping his ancestors alive by masterfully creating beautiful, compelling, and nostalgic paintings from this treasured collection of vintage photographs dating from 1912 to 1927. People wonder why this particular family was captured in such magnitude in over 300 pictures. It is a divine plan. The photographs, stories, and intimately executed paintings together produce a force so great that it forever binds the past with the present for this one family.

THE HYMAN COLLECTION

As we enter the new millennium, we tend to look back to the opening pages of the 20th century. Where were we one hundred years ago? What did we look like? What did we wear? How did we preserve our memories of those days and times?

Rick Hyman's family, who first traveled by covered wagons from Virginia to southern Texas after being freed from slavery, preserved family history as many of us do: by taking photographs of social occasions and by filling drawers with memorabilia ranging from dried corsages to jewelry.

In 1981, Rick Hyman discovered a treasure in the dresser drawer of a Texas aunt: 300 black-and-white photographs depicting the life of his ancestors who, one generation after being freed from slavery, prospered on their Texas oil land. Those 2,000 acres in Fayette County fed cattle and provided the Henderson Martin family with a horse and carriage, a stagecoach, four cars, plenty of silver, and fancy clothes and jewelry. Also found and remarkably preserved was vintage jewelry worn by his family in the late 1800s and early 1900s. These kinds of images, which capture the success of an African-American family in rural Texas, are rarely seen, if ever, from this time period. The photos and jewelry are now part of the Hyman Collection.

CATALOGING AND SHARING THE COLLECTION

Hyman is eager to share this rare glimpse of African-American life in the 1920s—life beyond the glitz of the Harlem Renaissance that so often depicts the culture during that era. Hyman's collection includes photos of students outside a rural schoolhouse, men and women dressed up for church and social functions, and men working on prized automobiles. Hyman's great-grandfather, Henderson Martin, owned four cars, driving a different one to church each Sunday for a month.

Hyman has carefully cataloged the well-preserved black-and-white vintage photographs, some with postcard backings. He has begun a second level of preservation by painting the variously sized photos in vibrant acrylic on canvas. His rare art form captures the ironies of the time: the formal dresses and Model-T Ford against a rural backdrop, the financial success of a family with their feet barely out of slavery, and the proud look that was 40 years ahead of the black pride movement in America. The jewelry worn by women in the photos and paintings further illustrates the wealth and success of the family. Fifty-four necklaces, bracelets, and other pieces in the Hyman Collection, most dating from the late 1800s to the early and mid-1900s, have been appraised and cataloged.

Hyman takes his family heritage and his country's history quite seriously. He wants to tell his family's history because it is an American story that has not been told. In *My Three Ancestors*, an acrylic and fabric quilt (55 inches x 65 inches), he recreates a story told to him (and recorded on audio tape) by a Texas cousin, Mamie Paige White. She recounts how her great-grandfather sat her down on the floor with other children and told them of his experiences during slavery and after emancipation. He told them how, as a freed slave, he drove one of the four wagons, consisting entirely of Hyman ancestors, in the wagon train. He described how first, they were attacked by Native Americans, and then later they were befriended by them and taught how to survive in the wilderness. These oral histories, like the photographs, provide substance and soul for painting the family history.

THE ARTIST AND EXHIBITS FEATURING HIS WORK

Before committing himself to preserving the 300 photos on canvas, Hyman painted (and still does) landscapes, jazz artists, and abstract images. It is the bloodline, Hyman says, that inspires his family paintings. He feels connected to his family ancestry and his country's history as he captures a different space and time on canvas. Hyman's work has even been recognized by Bill Cosby. A print of Hyman's first historical family portrait painting, *My Texas Family*, was hanging on the living room wall set of Cosby's prime-time sitcom. The Virginia Museum of Fine Arts is sponsoring a three-year traveling exhibition of Hyman's historical family series, entitled "The Riches of Family: An American Journey from Slavery to Prosperity," which is currently touring museums across the country. If you would like information on how you can bring this exhibit to your institution, museum, or gallery, contact Eileen Mott at the Virginia Museum of Fine Arts in Richmond at (804) 204-2682, email: emott@vmfa.state.va.us.

We almost locked away the photos and jewelry and just passed them on to our children, but because of the rich and rare legacy of our family, we wanted to share the collection. We share it with you now as you travel back in time on this journey with *My Texas Family*.

Chapter One

RICK HYMAN'S STORY

I have been blessed with knowing a tremendous amount of family history, whereas so many of us have not been and may never know very much at all about our family's past. I am still researching what happened in Africa, where some of my ancestors first originated, and what happened during the relationship between my great-great-grandfather, Cezar Martin, who was a slave in Virginia, and his son, Henderson Martin. To satisfy my appetite for the missing information and to release my feelings and emotions with this small, but precious corridor of time, I have created a short story of an imagined relationship between my great-great-grandfather, Cezar, and my great-grandfather, Henderson Martin. I can only imagine now what my experience would have been like had I known my great-grandfather personally.

My great-great-grandfather, Cezar Martin, told his son, Henderson Martin, who was six years old at the time, that we came from West Africa and that we were born of a rich and noble heritage. For centuries our family raised cattle and owned land as far as we could see. Cezar told Henderson to always own land, as much as you can get, because the more land you own the more nature is on it and the closer you are to God. He taught Henderson many family values, such as to always respect elders and your family. Cezar taught Henderson some of what he learned in Africa about animals, how to raise them and get them to obey and know that you are their master. He said if you whisper magical words into an animal's left ear, cattle or horses, even dogs, will be trained. Cezar even told him a story of how he once kept and trained a white tiger in Africa by doing the same thing. He claimed he could walk through a pack of tigers or lions on the prairie and would yell a few words out loud and they would all lie down when he passed.

I missed learning from Henderson how to be a farmer. When he was born in Texas in 1866, he was born into freedom. His mother and daddy would sing songs every night and pray many times throughout the day. The desire to always pray and sing songs remained with him all his life.

As a kid, Native Americans taught Henderson about the land. They told him that every tree and animal in the forest had a name and would talk to him if he would be quiet and listen. Henderson used to be woken up at 4:30 every morning by the

Kamberi Village, *by Rick Hyman, 1997. (Acrylic on canvas.)*

birds who seemed to always come near his window and sing. He just knew they were talking to him, telling him to wake up. Every time he would eat bread at a meal he would leave the corner or part of the crust and afterwards toss it outside for the birds to eat. His daddy told him that he would be blessed because he was giving back to nature. He also told Henderson that one day people would try to buy the land that they were living on but to never sell it. They would want it because it has lakes of oil underground, and the white man would use it for fuel one day. Henderson never forgot this, and eventually took the opportunity to own some of this land. He learned to pick cotton at the age of five. He was used to hard work and being out in the sun all day. My great-granddaddy was a real outdoorsman and a great horticulturalist.

When 1900 rolled, he was about 30 years old. Everybody used to wonder if the world was going to end. Some people in church just knew that Jesus was going to come back. They used to say this because of the way times were for blacks, and since slavery had just ended some 30 years before, Henderson's life was one of happiness and joy. No matter what the situation, he always looked on the brighter side of things, knowing that God and nature would take care of him no matter what. He used to say that God made the beautiful sky with clouds and sunsets, and sunrises and lovely colors to entertain us with every day of our lives.

Four-year-old Bruce Hyman Jr. (left) and his two-and-a-half-year-old brother, Rick Hyman (right), play cowboys at their home in Washington, D.C., in 1956.

I always wanted to be a cowboy. But when I learned that my mother's family owned oil property, I felt special. Not just oil property, but over 2,000 acres of oil property in the late 1800s and early 1900s. I told my mother that she was born with a silver spoon in her mouth. My grandparents died in 1975 and my mother's sister, Gussie Lee, died in 1981. It was after her death that my mother and I found the 300 photographs tucked away in a dresser drawer.

Every time I look at the pictures I see Henderson Martin with his cowboy hat on and never smiling. He looked mean, ornery, and like he "wouldn't take no bull from nobody." There was an air about him. Just looking at his picture and other pictures of my great aunts and cousins and uncles, you can see that they had a look that they had seen some truly hard times, extremely hard times facing tremendous obstacles, like bad snow storms and trying to stay warm on a huge farm out in Texas in the 1900s. I'm sure that Henderson had to worry about keeping his beautiful cattle alive, along with his turkeys, pigs, and crops such as corn and potatoes. He had to be aware and concerned about all of this, at a time in history when he and my ancestors did not depend on anyone else to keep them alive except God first and the farm second. My cousin Mamie White told me that the only thing that Henderson Martin would buy from the store was baking soda and salt. He grew everything else himself.

My mother used to tell me stories of all the silver Henderson had and about his stagecoach. This made me see my great-granddaddy as some type of superman for a black man during this time in American history in the South. My great-grandpa had to possess some type of congenial personality to get along with people of all different races just to survive. For a black man during this time period to acquire and hold onto so much really makes me feel like I should be proud to be related.

In my family pictures, people have a look on their faces as if they are saying, "we made it through slavery and see us, we are still here."

In 1984 I took a trip with my mother, Ida Mae Johnson Hyman, who was about 63 at the time, and our cousin Bernice McLaughlin and his wife, Evelyn, to Round Top, Texas, to see Great-granddaddy Henderson Martin's ranch, or as my mother used to call it, the Estate. I used to always wonder why she called it an estate. The only estates that I knew of were places like the television oil billionaire J.R. Ewing's ranch in South Fork (near Dallas), or the other oil millionaires, the Beverly Hillbillies. It's funny, but isn't it a coincidence that these family estates were acquired through oil money? Perhaps my mother was trying to tell me something but just did not know how to do so. She never told me that great-grandpa had oil on his property. I was so excited and overjoyed because I felt that this was a once in a lifetime opportunity to see where my mother's family came from and to see their oil property. I used to tell myself, "Rick, you know that very few African Americans can say that their ancestors owned oil property."

Rick Hyman (left) and friend, Mike Coleman, on the way to church on Sunday morning. They are standing on the porch of Hyman's grandfather's house (the Johnsons) on Delano Street (Ward Three) in Houston in the 1980s.

25

Rick Hyman and his uncle Raymond Martin (grandson of Henderson Martin) at Marjorie Martin Tones's home in Houston. This photo was taken in June 1996.

While driving up there all I could think about was how God was with us and how he was blessing me with this opportunity. Bernice was having a good time telling me about the fun they had as kids growing up. I guess he and all of us were just enjoying the ride and the fresh air and the countryside.

After driving for about an hour I began to see large herds of cattle on huge ranches and I could not help but wonder if this was what my great-granddaddy's farm looked like. It was beautiful countryside with huge farms as far as the eye could see. But once we got about 100 miles away from the estate, we were driving on a two-lane road and all I could see was lots of land with huge oil wells on both sides of the road. The air smelled of petroleum. It was not an offensive smell, but rather a heavy aroma. I guess it was not offensive to me because I was thinking about all of the money these people who owned the wells were getting. The excitement and intensity grew the closer we got to his land. There were oil trucks passing us by, large tankers the size of 18 wheelers. Once we arrived at the property we pulled over and got out at the gate. It was a sunny day with blue skies and a few clouds. It was perfect and I felt a breeze as we got out of the car. I knew that that breeze was the spirit of Henderson and the other family members who once lived and worked this land.

There was a lock on the gate to the land, but Bernice said, "You're looking at the land that your great-granddaddy owned." Ma even pointed out where the house used to be. There were no oil wells on the land, and I was glad because I wanted to see it as it used to be or as close to the way it was. There were oil wells on both sides of the property and across the street.

The highway in front of the property was covered with mud and black tire tracks left by the oil trucks transporting oil off the surrounding properties.

It was overwhelming for me to see one of these oil trucks leaving from the ranch next to ours. There was a white man driving the truck. I felt kind of funny inside, a sense of resentment because I knew that this was supposed to be happening on our estate too. We were supposed to be driving up to this property in a chauffeured limousine drinking champagne. My mother used to play on this land as a little girl all the time.

The first time I found out about oil on my great-granddaddy's land was in 1982, when I was about 34 years old. A feeling went through me that I cannot put into words. My cousin Bernice is the one who told me. My mother moved away from Texas in her early 20s after she graduated from Wiley College in Marshall, Texas. She married and moved to Washington, D.C.

Once I started studying to get a real estate license in 1976, I began to ask questions and wanted to know more about the estate and all the property that my great-granddaddy owned. My mother always called her sister in Texas, but Gussie did not want to tell my mother anything about the property. We tried and tried. It was around this same time in 1974 that the family began to sell off some of their pieces of the remaining 68 acres that Henderson had purchased. Mother used to tell me that Aunt Gussie would not tell her anything or even where the will was to their daddy's house because my mother moved so far away and left their parents and did not come back for over 40 years except to visit. Mother replied, "I'm married and I have to take care of my husband and our two kids." Talking about this oil property with relatives really took courage on my part. It was funny, but I felt embarrassed to ask my relatives about it because I was young at the time. I guess I felt that I was nosing into somebody else's business since I did not grow up in Texas.

I remember Bernice telling me that when he was a young boy he asked Aunt Bessie (Henderson Martin's daughter) about her father's 2,000 acres of oil land and she told him, "Shut up, don't you talk about that." He told me they were so secretive, as if they were trying to hide something. I'm sure it struck a nerve in the people I asked too, but I felt that I was not out of place and, being a grown man, I needed to know about my family's estate.

After we left great-granddaddy's old ranch, we drove into the town of La Grange, Texas. We rode around and bought some barbecue from a butcher's shop. While walking, Bernice stopped and began to tell me about an incident that happened in this town around 1891. At that time, Henderson Martin was in his mid-20s. I began to just let my mind wander and tried to picture him a young man, full of energy, wearing his boots all the way to his knees and his silver Belly cowboy hat, riding into town on his beautiful horse. As he rode into the main street of town he saw some white men. There was one white man who approached him as he walked toward the feed store after he tied his horse up. The man was tall with black hair, a thick mustache, and piercing steel blue eyes as if he could look right through you. All of the other eight or nine men watching knew what one of them (I'll call him Dick) was going to do because they had seen him do this to other blacks in town before, but they had never met Henderson.

Some of the women in town gathered around as Dick stood in front of Henderson, cutting right in front of his path as he walked up the dusty street. He asked him what he was doing in town. He came so close that Henderson could smell Dick's cigar smoke. Henderson did not back down. He told the man that he was going to the feed store and he looked Dick straight in the eyes without blinking, his head held high. Dick told him that he heard that colored people could dance real good and that the townspeople always needed to see a new colored man come to town and dance before he could walk around. Henderson did not move until Dick pulled his gun out of his holster on his left side and pointed the long shiny dark barrel at Henderson's feet. It was about mid-day and the sunlight was reflecting off the shiny chrome of the pistol. Suddenly Dick yelled, "I said dance, nigger, dance," and he let off all six rounds in his gun. So Henderson danced. A few small boys began to run after they heard the loud gunshots and the crowd of about 20 who had formed a circle around them started laughing at the way Henderson was dancing. At first, he got embarrassed for having to dance. And then he got angry and felt he had to do something about this. It hurt his pride to dance and put on a show for people. Dick thought Henderson was going to back up or run. Then suddenly, Henderson turned to Dick and said, "Now its your turn to dance." Dick did not know that Henderson always carried a short rifle hidden in his waist band. Dick told Henderson, "Nigger, don't you get smart with me" and started to walk towards Henderson. Then Henderson drew his short rifle and shot Dick in the chest. The crowd was shocked. Dick fell to the ground instantly holding his chest with both of his hands, his black cowboy hat flying off his head. This shot seemed to be louder than the others. There was a second of silence in which Henderson turned around real fast, his short rifle still smoking. Everybody ran. He then jumped on his horse and quickly rode out of town heading straight to the Martin Liggons ranch. The sheriff and the posse in town jumped on their horses and chased Henderson to the Liggons ranch. But they did not catch him. Back then you could do anything to anybody in town, but once you got back to the farm nobody was going to bother you there.

Old Man Liggons (a white man) killed several men himself. He had quite a reputation. Nobody was going to come up on his farm and bother Henderson or anybody else, not even the sheriff. I guess Henderson got his meanness and some of his ways from Martin Liggons, because he helped raise him. When I heard this story I tried to imagine the courage it must have taken to shoot a white man during that time in the South. What nerve. I'm sure a lot of thoughts were going through his mind before he did it, but I guess survival came first. I can imagine how I would have felt if I was told this story the other way around and somebody said he danced and then ran away without putting up a glorious fight. I bet a lot of thoughts were going through Henderson's head as he was riding away from town, chased by some of the men on their horses until he got to the Liggons farm.

St. Paul's AME Church dates back to 1852–53. It is the oldest church in La Grange and one of the oldest in Texas. Hyman's cousin Mamie recalls, "Morris Brown AME Church (Warrenton), Round Top Baptist Church, and other black churches were all built around the same time, sometime around the 1860s. It was your (and my) ancestors who founded Morris Brown AME Church. They bought land for their church from white folks. But when the blacks started moving toward the towns, and the congregation of Morris Brown got low, they sold the land back to the whites. Some of the congregation merged with the St. Paul AME Church, and some joined up with Bassady AME Church." (Bassady was located between Giddings and La Grange.)

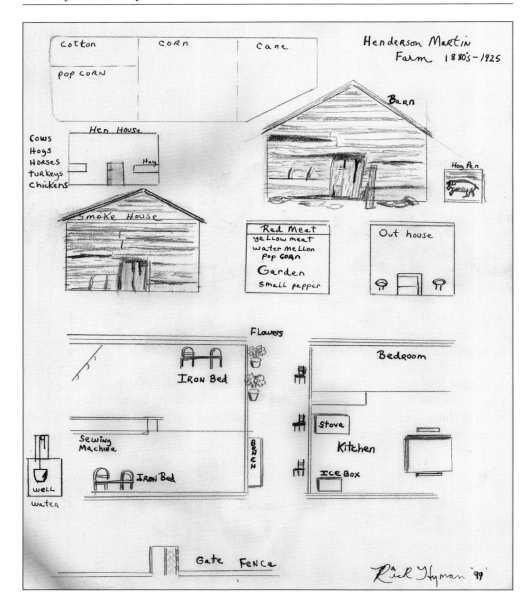

The labels in the sketch read:

Cotton   Corn   Cane

Pop Corn

Henderson Martin Farm 1880's – 1925

Barn

Cows Hogs Horses turkeys Chickens

Hen House   Hay

Hog Pen

Smoke House

Red Meat
yellow meat
water mellon
pop corn
Garden
small pepper

Out house

Flowers

Iron Bed

Bedroom

Sewing Machine

Bench

Stove

Kitchen

Iron Bed

Well water

Ice Box

Gate   Fence

Rick Hyman '99

The original sketch of the Henderson Martin farm was drawn by his granddaughter, Eliza Martin Calhoun, who spent a lot of time there as a young girl. When she drew the first diagram on July 1, 1998, she remembered that in the Henderson Martin farmhouse, they had no closets to hang their clothes. So, at the corner of the bedroom (see diagram), they put a nail in two walls and tied a piece of wire to connect them. Then they would lay the clothes over the wire and throw a sheet over the whole thing to cover it up. This was their closet, to the left of the iron bed. The above sketch was redrawn from the original by Henderson Martin's great-grandson, artist Rick Hyman.

After Bernice told me this story, we got in the car and headed back to Houston. What a day it was, seeing great-granddaddy's estate with my mother and cousins—the estate I had heard so much about. I got a chance to see where I came from.

We were traveling east from Round Top on a two-lane highway. I was driving and Bernice was sitting next to me in the front seat when I looked to my right and saw a train, an old-timey looking locomotive train traveling parallel to our car headed in the same direction about 20 or 30 yards to my right. As I continued to look at the train, I yelled and pointed as I noticed a horse that was running in the same direction in between our car and the train. Not just a common horse, but a beautiful, muscular, black stallion. Both the train and our vehicle were traveling about 60 miles an hour, but the horse was keeping up with us. How mystical this was to see only minutes after visiting my great-granddaddy's estate. At first I wondered if the horse had broken loose from being tied up in one of the train cars, but I changed my mind in a few minutes. I say this because the horse was running as if he knew us, as if he knew what he was doing. He continued to keep in stride with our car and the train. Why? All four of us in the car could not believe our eyes. I was trying to keep the car in the middle of the road and yet watch this event at the same time. I wondered to myself, "how is this going to end?" Then after about six or seven minutes, the horse sped up, outrunning our car and the train, and suddenly decided to make a sharp left turn. When it did this I had to stop my car because it ran right in front of our vehicle across the highway. But when it was directly in front of our car, it turned its head to the left and looked me right in the eye. Was this a message? I believe it was. I felt that this was one of the spirits from my family's past letting us know that they realized who we were and that they are still with us.

Chapter Two

ORAL HISTORIES

ILLUSTRATED BY THE HYMAN FAMILY PHOTOGRAPHS (1912–1927)

Rick Hyman's grandfather, Ell Johnson, appears in the center of this photograph.

My Texas Family. *(Acrylic on canvas, 30 in. x 40 in.) For the color representation, please turn to p. 116.*

Pictured from left to right are Henderson Martin, Lizzie Martin (Henderson's wife), and their daughter Cornelius, a schoolteacher, on their estate in Warrenton, Texas, in 1925. Another daughter, Tiny, sits inside the car. This photograph was the inspiration for Hyman's first historical painting, My Texas Family.

CONVERSATIONS WITH COUSIN MAMIE:
The Covered Wagon Journey to Texas

Rick: This conversation took place with my cousin, Mamie Paige White, in Houston in 1997. In it, she described the journey my ancestors took from Virginia to Texas. Mamie's mother was Clara Jones Simmons. Her family name was Roberson, which was the name of their slave master. Slaves came from Virginia, South Carolina, and Georgia, and traveled to Texas through Burton in a covered wagon train. Some freed slaves came on steamboats by water, entering Texas through Galveston. Grandpa Poleon (Mamie's great-grandfather) was married to Lizzie Roberson, and together they drove one of the wagons. He and his wife took turns driving. Mamie said that Poleon was a short man. The travelers were all former slaves.

Mamie: The drug store in La Grange was owned by the Meyenburgs. They were those slave master's descendants. Their nephew ran Meyenburg's.

Meyenburg, his daddy's people, were former owners of slaves. Some of our relatives were slaves of Meyenburg. One hundred and twenty people made it to Texas on this wagon train. Some died along the way. I was six years old when Mama's grandfather died. I remember he used to sit us children down on the flo' telling us about this. Four wagons made it to Texas. Then some more came behind them. But four wagons made it to Texas first. First it was Mama's mother and father (the Robersons), then the Ligons and the Martins. Mama married Fred Jones, and her mother married a Jones. That made both of their last names Jones.

Before they left Virginia, the canvas cloth for the covered wagon came over on a boat. The slaves knew how to sew so they sewed tents and canvas cloths together. The sheets or the cloth for the top of the covered wagons looked a khaki color, but they were moss green or gray after they were dyed. They put walnuts in a big old black wash pot to dye to make it different colors so they could distinguish it from other stuff and to get it the color they wanted. When they arrived in Texas the top of the covered wagons had bleached to a beige color; we called it eggshell white.

The women had big bonnets and wore long dresses that touched the top of their shoes because they were so long. The women would wear the big bonnets and would drive them old wagons like the men. After they got ambushed, some of the former slave owners took over the slaves and recaptured them after they were free because they did not want them to come to Texas. Some of them got ambushed, some of them got killed.

Making Our Way to Something Better. *(Acrylic on canvas, 7 ft. x 8 ft.) Please see p. 122 for the color representation of this painting.*

Rick Hyman's relatives, including his great-aunt, Margaret Martin (far left), stand beside a Cadillac in Hyde Park. Not far from Austin, this park was a popular place for African Americans to gather for outings or to drive their automobiles.

Ellen Martin Johnson holds her baby daughter, Ida Mae Johnson Hyman, in La Grange. Other relatives, Mabel, Alice, and Nora, are also pictured. Hyman reproduced this image as a color painting entitled From These Beginnings, *which can be seen on p. 127 of this book.*

Elvin Jones sits outside on Henderson Martin's farm. Behind him, a washtub hangs on the side of the barn. The crops, probably corn, are visible in the background.

The Indians shot one lady's husband with an arrow and killed him. After that they got to be friends with the Indians, because the Indians really thought that these people were going to harm them. But after they found out that these people weren't going to harm them, they became friends and even taught them how to survive in the wilderness. If it had not been for the Indians, these people would never have made it to Texas. They did not know nothing about the wilderness, they did not have no food, nothing. Only thing they ate was wild stuff, what they would catch out in the woods, armadillos, squirrels, wild hogs, deer. That's what they had to live off of. See those Indians taught them how to live off that.

One of the lady's husbands was shot with the arrow, so she brought that dead man into Texas. He was still on the wagon dead and she brought him to Texas. See it was cold then and people used salt, like table salt, and matches, that's how they used to embalm people. America did not know anything about embalming at this time. In Texas, embalming first came out in 1930. The embalmer was John Pennigraph. He was taking black folks in a lodge and embalming them.

Rick Hyman's great-aunts—Margaret Martin (left) and her sister, Bessie Martin (right)—at Hyde Park. They are standing behind a Model-T Ford.

This image was sent on a postcard from Etnar Ligons to Ell Johnson in about 1916.

Ida Mae Johnson at about 18 months old outside of her home in La Grange. Photo c. 1925.

Ida Mae and Gussie Lee with their uncle, Connie Lee Martin.

Elvin Jones (Henderson Martin's son-in-law) was Mamie Paige White's Uncle Monk.

One of the Martin daughters stands with a family car. The tag number is 275-399 TX.

Baby Ida Mae and her sister, Gussie Lee, sit with their aunt, Margaret (Tiny) Martin Jones, at Henderson Martin's house. Bessie Martin is standing in the door.

Ethel Mae (left) and Lullaby Martin stand on a rug made from a pick sack, a bag in which cotton was placed after being picked.

The lady was the leader of the wagon then, 'cause after her husband, who was the leader of the wagon, got killed, the rest of them in the wagons were women and children. This was one of our family members that drove this wagon train into Texas; Grandma and them was in the front wagon, the Martins were in the second, and the Ligons were in the third. Your great-grandfather's people were Martins, Mama and them were Robersons, then there was another set that were Ligons (kinfolk).

Rick: Why did they choose Texas?

Mamie: When they came to Texas, they were going to go on a farm. This farm was called Hellers Farm. Hellers's relatives had had some slaves over there [in Virginia]. This is where they settled, that farm was out in Walhalla Edition, and all you could see was nothing but land, land, land. It was a few houses and they eventually had a church house, and they used this as a school for years and years. It was a little old white church, the littlest church in Texas. Then they finally built a school, out from Warrenton, Texas. This is where your grandfather's people are from—Hellers Farm.

Hellers had a couple of farms, one in Round Top and one in Warrenton. He had Negroes out there. One of the ex-slave masters had bought land in Texas. This is where the ex-slave relatives were going. Old man Heller was white and his daddy or grandfather or somebody owned slaves. That was the reason they were coming to Texas. They came to Texas as free people, those that made it here. They started out for Texas cause one of the ex-slave boss's relatives had bought land in Texas.

Rick: But was it some tough times?

Mamie: It was some hard times; wasn't no tough times, it was hard, hard times. For breakfast they would eat anything they could get their hands on. They did not have no specialty. They would kill rabbits. I guess they would barbecue them or roast them out there, and whatever was left they ate the next day until they caught something else. They tell me that they would take the hide, like from them coons and things and dry them and make shoes out of them. They ate them coons, you know.

Rick: Do we have any Native American blood in our family?

Mamie: Half of your family is part Indian. Don't you see your high cheekbones? Where do you think you got your high cheekbones from? You know them people got cross-breeded out there in them woods. I don't know what tribe of Indians. There was plenty of Indian territory. Your family's wagon train was ambushed in Oklahoma by the Indians.

Rick: Did the men have any rifles or guns as they were traveling?

Mamie: Only thing they had that I heard my Grandpa say was about four guns; there was a double-barreled shotgun in each wagon. That's what my great grandfather told me. That's what they had and that's what they would kill with until them Indians came after them. That's the reason that man was shot with an arrow driving the wagon because he had this gun on the front of the wagon. They call it a spring seat, where the men and one of the women would ride up there with the husband. You see, when that man got tired of driving, the woman would drive,

Etnar Gates and her children. In the background of the image on the left are Henderson Martin's fields and a fire pit where the family may have warmed up their food or drinks.

Young girls on the ranch in La Grange. All of these ladies knew how to ride a horse. The one standing to the right aims her rifle.

and then they would camp over night in different areas, see, cause they could not come just straight on, or just ride, ride, ride—they had to let those mules or horses rest, whatever they were driving, but I don't believe they had any horses. They probably had a couple of horses because somebody had to go along and kind of scout, you know.

Rick: Did they have mules when they left slavery?

Mamie: Oh yes, definitely.

Rick: Did they ever have to shoot anybody with the guns as they were traveling?

Mamie: Now, I did not hear them say that they did, Grandpa didn't say. You see, they had had enough of killing and beating on the slave plantations. He said when they came off the slave farm, they had seen enough of how people beat up the slaves until they would die and all that. They had enough of that, he said.

Rick: What did the women wear?

Mamie: Bonnets and long dresses, and also aprons. The dresses and aprons would come down to the ground just covering their shoes.

Rick: Did they go to church back then?

Mamie: You know them people couldn't go to no church back then! They would have different meetings and things amongst themselves. They would have prayer meetings and pray to the good Lord above, cause that's the way they kept themselves together to survive, where they were. Because it was hard. Because I heard Grandpa say they used to be out in the field around those hollow logs and how they got happy and get the spirit and put their heads up in the end of those logs and shout so that the massa would not hear them. You know the log was hollow, so when they shouted the massa couldn't hear them. The log would muffle the sound. The massa would not let them worship the Lord openly, you know.

Rick: Every time I hear the story about this wagon train journey, my heart is beating fast and my brain is almost tired because physically I feel as though I am right there on the journey with my ancestors. I clearly see every wagon, every tree, every person, and I listen and just go back in time to 1863. I created the painting *Making Our Way to Something Better* (see p. 122 for the color representation) after Mamie told me this story about my family traveling in the covered wagons. I painted it as it was told to me, and when I found out that the woman who led the wagons into Texas was one of my relatives, it just became so clear that she must not be forgotten. This legacy must be told. I was told this story at the age of 44 and had never seen any images of African Americans in covered wagons before. I never saw this in my school books. So I am painting many scenes of history I never saw when I was in school. I pray that this book will be used in the classrooms, museums, and other institutions. It is not meant to offend any race of people; it is just meant to convey the events and history of one of the first prosperous black families in Texas as it happened during our country's early history.

The Early Years in La Grange

Mamie: I was born outside of La Grange and went to school in Walhalla, that's why I know so much about this Hellers Farm. Some of my first years in elementary school were in Walhalla. It was nice out in the country, there was an old gin out there. It was Walhalla where they first had church when they came to Texas. There was a well, they would put rope on a chain and draw this water out of the well. Like when they went to church, they would put them wagon sheets over the wagon so they wouldn't get wet or the sun wouldn't shine on them. You could have four or five of those wagons with horses parked around the church, with the people climbing off the wagons and the children running and playing around in the yard. Then you could go on further out and have some cotton in a cotton field and have a wagon off in there.

Rick: What time period was this?

Mamie: Now, when I was a little girl . . . I was born in 1925, so that would have to be around 1935. They went to church in them wagons too. They didn't have cars then. They had to have two horses to a wagon, and then they had these buggies. You know what buggies are? Some people were up in a little bit higher class than others, and they had what you call a surreys. It had two seats to it, fringes around the top, and then they drew two horses to that. The others who weren't up in that higher class didn't have fringes around their buggies. Some of the wagons were open in the back; some would put a wagon seat over the top of 'em, like these wagons that they had in slavery.

Rick: Like the buckboard wagons?

Mamie: Uh huh. The man would have to sit up there in the front and he drove, but the children and the wives would be back in the wagon part.

Rick: Did they have seats in the back of the wagon?

Mamie: Yeah, they had to put chairs in the back for the older people and the children.

Rick: And the cotton would be towards the back of the church?

Mamie: The cotton would be off from the church. You know they had the cemetery on the church grounds. And there would be a road in between the church and the cotton. You could see this cotton way down, you could just look across the viewing place. You could see the people in the cotton fields with the cotton sacks picking cotton and all that stuff. That's what I saw when I went to church. And then on through the week when they went to the store, you'd see people coming to the store or either they'd be out there in the fields.

Rick: What was the name of the church?

Mamie: Morris Brown AME Church in Walhalla.

Yesteryear. *(Acrylic on canvas, 36 in. x 48 in.) Please see p. 123 for the color representation.*

Rick Hyman's great uncles, Willie and Raymond Martin, pose on the Martin ranch with a Model T Ford. For a recent picture of these two, please turn to the chapter featuring Henderson Martin's descendants.

Katie Smith, a relative, in Warrenton, Texas.

Lullaby Martin, Rick Hyman's great-aunt.

Connie Lee Martin was Rick Hyman's great-uncle and Henderson Martin's son. He helped his dad on his ranch.

Rick Hyman's great-aunt, Ethel Mae Martin Dobbins, poses on her daddy's ranch.

From left to right are James Clark of Giddings, Leo Hawkins of Victoria, and Mr. Black of Austin.

Margaret Martin Jones and Elvin Jones, after their wedding.

Rick: And what part of Texas was that?

Mamie: Fayette County, sho' was.

Rick: I remember that story you told me back in Virginia about old man Roberson not letting the people have church so they had to go out in the fields.

Mamie: Sho', they would have to go out in the fields, they betta get out there. They couldn't have no church when it was slavery times, they had to have it in the field. And they betta not get too loud.

Rick: And they were picking cotton and all?

Mamie: They were picking cotton and cutting corn and everything, chopping corn. They planted corn and when it would get the hedge on it, they would cut the tops off and let them lay on the ground until they dried. Then they would feed them to the cattle in the winter time. You know, the massa wouldn't too much let them slaves go to town. When they did let them go, they couldn't come right up to the front of the store, they would have to wait until all the white people in there had gotten their groceries and stuff first, and then them slaves that was the house slaves (they was the ones that could go to town) could buy things in the store.

Rick: But the other slaves couldn't come to town?

Mamie: No, they was what you call field slaves. They wouldn't allow them, but the slave women who would work in the massa men's house, they could go to town.

Rick: And how did they get to town?

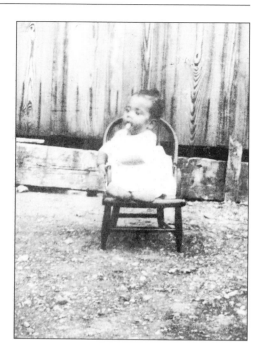

Ida Mae Johnson (Rick Hyman's mother) on the Martin Ranch in 1925.

Lullaby Martin (left) and Etnar Gates (right) were not only cousins, but were also the best of friends.

Ell Johnson, Rick Hyman's grandfather.

Ms. Irene Brown's house in East Vine, La Grange. When Aunt Serge came to visit, she used to stay with them.

Mamie: Massa and them would let the cook, that man, have a wagon and he would carry them cooks and the housekeepers to town in the wagon.

Rick: The man who drove the wagon, was he a black or white man?

Mamie: Now you know that white man wouldn't let no white man carry them negroes to town. You know that was another black man.

Rick: So there was a black man in the house?

Mamie: We call him a butler nowadays. He was the house man. He shined Massa's shoes, and helped dress Massa and kept up Massa's clothes, the old slave Massa's clothes. He kept his house all neat and, you know, fancy.

Rick: How was he dressed?

Mamie: I imagine he had overalls or khakis on. He probably wore some black or navy blue pants with a belt, a nice shirt and tie.

Rick: And what did the women wear?

Mamie: Them old long funny-made dresses with them aprons on it and bonnets.

Rick: And they would go to the back door of the feed place?

Mamie: They sho' couldn't come in the front.

Rick: And they would get food and supplies and stuff for the master?

Mamie: That's right. They know what they'd cook, so they had to go to the store.

Rick: And is this the information that Mr. Poleon told you?

Mamie: Grandpa Poleon told us all that, cause see, Grandma Lizzie and Grandpa Poleon were slaves when they come to Texas. See, Mr. Meyenburg in La Grange had a drugstore there, but they had a farm also out there in the country and they carried those Negroes to the farm, you know. And he was nice enough to give the Negroes, Grandpa and Grandma Lizzie, ten acres of land out there in the country, cause he wasn't gonna have them in town. Cause you know when he come from Virginia, he wasn't gonna have them 'niggas' up in town, they may "learn" something.

Rick: So he was in Virginia with them?

Mamie: Ah yeah, he was one of the massas. It was him or his daddy.

Rick: What was his name again?

Mamie: Meyenburg. That's who brought them to Texas. Grandpa Roberson, they call him Poleon Roberson, but anyway, he said there were four wagons that came with them. And he said some of the people got sick. Some of them died along the way, but they finally made it to Texas. See, that's where the nineteenth of June originated.

Rick: Now this was right after the slaves were freed?

Mamie: Yeah.

Rick: You say this is Meyenburg's daddy who had a plantation?

Mamie: That's right, I don't know the whole name, if it was George Meyenburg or what, but I know he had a plantation up there, cause Grandpa Poleon used to talk about it all the time. When he used to come to La Grange with mama's daddy, Fred Jones, mama's daddy was what they called a teamster—he drove a wagon and he would get food and supplies for the stores out there in Warrenton, and he would bring them out there to the stores. He would bring Grandpa Poleon to town with him all the time, occasionally, you know when he was up to it.

Rick: What did Grandpa Poleon look like?

Mamie: He was a little short dark man, a nice looking man. But his wife was a big tall woman, with a light complexion and pretty long hair.

Rick: What were your favorite sweets when you were growing up?

Mamie: Favorite sweets? Mother and them used to make sweet potato pies and old-fashioned tea cakes. People don't know nothing about old-fashioned tea cakes. They made them out of yeast, sugar, butter, milk, flour, nutmeg, and put cinnamon on top. Momma and them used to make tea cakes and put them in a flower sack, a 48 pound flour sack.

Rick: Could the women ride horses back then?

Mamie: All the girls were cowgirls. These women could ride a horse or mule better than you could. Ride 'em sideways, man! That's the way you went to the mailboxes. The mailbox was so far from the house that you had to ride the horse to get there. I'm telling you about the time around 1865 after slavery. After the Negroes started going to school a little while, they started migrating to town. They came here to Houston to what they called the Fourth Ward. That was almost a colony. That's where all the Negroes who came to Houston would settle. They had everything: they had their cleaners, their stores, and everything. In 1921, they started embalming down here. But in a little place like La Grange it didn't start till the 1930s. But in the cities down here, like Houston, embalming started in the '20s. It all started in the Fourth Ward. There's an old church in the Fourth Ward over there called Antioch Baptist Church—it's over a hundred years old. That's where a lot of

Ethel Martin, Rick Hyman's great aunt, is pictured in her lace-up, high-top shoes, which were either black or brown.

Margaret Martin, Rick Hyman's great aunt, at Hyde Park.

those ex-slaves went, to this church. When the wagon sheets faded and got real thin, that's when the old people took them and made dresses out of them. That's where that old black walnut and hickory nut thing came in. They would put that in the pot with the wagon sheets and dye them, and then they'd make their dresses out of them.

Rick: This would happen after they took them off the wagons?

Mamie: That's right, cause after a length of time they would wear down from the wagon path and the weather. See, cause if you just put something outside out in the weather and let it stay for a long time, you'll see how it wears down. My daddy's name was James Lee Paige. His father's name was Andrew Paige. Raymond Martin and I are first cousins. Their mama and my daddy were sister and brother. When the blacks had land up in La Grange and Warrenton, they did not know they had minerals under it. When they started drilling those oil wells they would go under the ground and steal oil. In those days, black folks did not know to ask for their mineral rights, cause nobody told them. That's the reason they don't have anything. A lot of them black folks didn't know they had oil on their property til it was all gone. But today we demand our mineral rights. We black folks have come a long way by the grace of the good Lord.

Dealing with the Times

Mamie: Round Top built up a school from Round Top Church to keep Negroes from going to white schools in Waldecker. In the 1940s Mr. George Scott, Julian Brown, and William Collins had a strike at the school because we were getting secondhand books from white schools. Erias Roam and Mrs. Dobbins were the only two teachers teaching one hundred students. We were small when we went there. I went to a school behind Matt Rile Grocery store. The school went up to the ninth grade. Mrs. Hettie Dobbins taught there, and Mr. Hillard Harris was principal. It was overcrowded. Randolph High almost had a riot in La Grange.

Everybody sat out under an oak tree to protest because the school was full and overcrowded. It was cold that day. The NAACP came in there with the Masons to assist. They were all around the school and made sure Negroes would not go in there. All the cars were lined up. They were walking and riding. They got Mr. George Scott of the NAACP, and somebody from Austin came over. During this time I was ironing for a white woman, who told me that she did not mind if my children went to the all-white school in La Grange. I told her that I did not mind if her children or whites went to the La Grange school either, as I looked her in the eye. Needless to say, after making that statement, I lost my job ironing for her.

Far Left: Etnar Gates.
Left: Kate Smith.

Undefeated. *(Acrylic on canvas, 36 in. x 48 in.) Please see p. 118 for the color representation of this painting.*

The 1921 Spring Hill College women's basketball team. Ellen Martin is to the immediate right of the male coach.

Gussie C., Ellen, Serge, Bessie, Margaret, Ethel, and Tiny at home in Warrenton. They were all Rick Hyman's great aunts.

Ethel Mae Martin Dobbins sits on the side of her father's car. In later years, Rick and Ronda Hyman visited Ms. Dobbins several times at her home in Houston.

Gussie Lee Martin with Mabel Grant and Frankie Mae Holles of West Point, Texas.

This baptism scene took place at Kate Hole, off from a creek in Warrenton. The preacher and deacon are on the far left. Mr. Heller (white man on far right) owned the big plantation in town and was the son of the slave owner, "Old Man" Heller. His plantation was the place where Hyman's relatives first settled when they arrived in Texas. The fourth person from the left, the lady wearing a bonnet and peeking through the crowd, looks exactly like Rick Hyman's mother, Ida Mae Johnson Hyman, but she was only one year old at the time of this photo. This lady, and most of the others pictured, were probably ancestors of Rick Hyman.

I was determined to go to school. I sold my calf and Uncle Elvin Jones gave me a "yellin'." I was determined I was not going to live in La Grange. Mama's cousin, Effie Gilmore, was living in Third Ward. I finally got to rent a three-room shack in Houston for eight dollars a week. I went to nursing school and worked hard for three doctors. On Sundays we would relax and go different places. One Sunday, we went to Monument Hill, another Sunday towards Plum, Texas. Kate Hole was too far to walk. Kate Hole is the baptism place with a large pool of water in the river, where the pastor and other people are standing about to get baptized in the photo from our family album. Some times we would go down to the Flat or Acre.

My mother will be 98 years old on July 8th, 1999. She tells me that she is already one hundred years old, but I checked the birth records and she is 98 now.

Rick: When I first met Mamie and her mother at their home in Houston, I was amazed at how smooth her mother's dark skin was and her hands were so soft, like cotton. When Bernice told her that my grandfather was Ell Johnson from La Grange and that Henderson Martin was my great grandfather, Mamie's mother told me that she could look in my eyes and know who I was. She is very dark with keen features and her eyes are a blue grayish color.

She was bed-ridden and took my hand as I looked at her and she opened my right hand as if she was about to read my palm. She ran her thin, brown index finger along my palm's lifeline, and told me that I was going to live a long time. All of a sudden she took her fingers and smacked my palm, shouting, "now go and tell God's word!" I felt so special after this, as if I was supposed to be doing something great, or as if I have a calling now. Mamie has told me many times that the Lord probably wants me to preach his word. Mamie's mother was preaching in the pulpit all the way up to 92 years old.

Etnar Gates and family. The little boy on the right is standing tall on the running board of the Model T Ford.

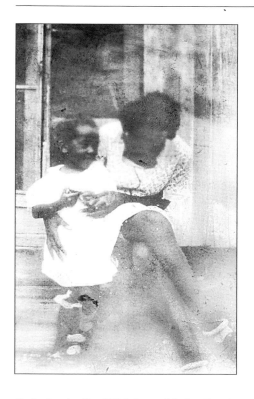

Ruby Louise Pool Wright and baby Gussie Lee Martin.

Mr. Black of Austin.

An unidentified little girl stands by a garden with a buckboard wagon in the background.

Little Ida Mae and Gussie Lee at home on the farm in La Grange.

A *Family of Church Builders and Preachers*

This conversation between Rick and cousin Mamie took place on June 22, 1999.

Rick: It seems as though religion was very strong in our family and I know your mother was preaching for years. Was there anything handed down that she might have told you that her great grandfather told her, you know, anything that was passed down regarding our family's special closeness to God?

Mamie: Yes, I tell you what, Mama's mother's husband, Poleon Roberson, was a preacher.

Rick: Was he?

Mamie: Uh huh. He couldn't read and he couldn't write, but let me tell you what, I was living when he died, I was five years old when Mama's mama's daddy died. He couldn't read and write, but he could tell you every scripture in the Bible; he knew 'em by heart. Now I don't know how he got 'em and how he learned it, but he could tell you every scripture of the Bible and what verse to find it in. He could come from Genesis and go all the way back to Revelations. . . and he couldn't read and write. Now you know God had to give that to that man.

Rick: Yeah, that's true. That is incredible.

Far Left: Hettie Dobbins (Ethel Martin Dobbins's in-law) was a teacher at Rock Hill School. The car's tag number is 353-659 TX.
Left: J.S. Campbell, a friend of the family, appears at a celebration or gathering at Hyde Park. This event probably took place after church on a Sunday.

Southern Gentlemen on a Sunday Afternoon. *(30 in. x 40 in.) Please see p. 119 for the color representation of this painting.*

These five distinguished gentlemen, including one clergyman, were attending their quarterly Methodist Church conference in Warrenton. Photo 1925.

Reverend Ruffins used to pastor at Cedar Grove Church. He drove a nice two-seated car and had a big "yellow" woman for a wife. One time, Reverend Ruffins and another man were drinking before church. While the Reverend was inside preaching up a storm at the pulpit one Sunday morning, the other man was reading scriptures, yelling them to the Reverend from the outside in back of the church, helping him preach.

Mamie: That was something, I'm telling you. There were only three churches, four, at that time in Fayette County that I know of. That was Round Top called Carl Baptist Church, and then it was another church called Big Spring Hill and in La Grange it was called the St. Paul AME Church. And out in the country they called it Morris Brown—Morris Brown AME Church.

Rick: Now is that the one our ancestors founded?

Mamie: That's the one that your ancestors built, Morris Brown AME Church, and if it was still going, it would be way up there in the hundreds. It would be over a hundred years old. Let me see, I would say about 125 or 130 years old.

Rick: But you were saying that your great grandfather, Poleon, was on the wagon train. Tell me about him preaching on the wagon train.

Mamie: Poleon would preach on the wagon train and they would all gather round the fire. You couldn't get too loud, cause they were coming through places, you know they weren't free, completely free, there were some places that they almost had to slip through. They had to have them brushes and things. They had to go and gather this stuff up and they would make a fire. They had to cook in those pots and things out in the open, over an open fire. They didn't have what you call furniture and things. That came later, in later years. Like you used to see your mama iron with the coals underneath. It was a round thing, like an ice cream thing, you put the irons on that. You couldn't get but two on there.

Rick: Now you said something about the reason for June 19th?

Beatrice Chanler married Guy Martin (Henderson Martin's son).

Sadie East Dobbins on the Martin farm.

Aunt Sergie and Aunt Bessie Martin were Rick Hyman's great-aunts. Here they stand in front of Mr. Martin's Model T Ford.

Bessie Martin sits in the driver's seat of the car.

Tom Thumb wedding. The event was used to raise money for the church or school, in addition to allowing young children to experience a wedding.

Mamie: Wait a minute, let me come on, let me come on about this 19th of June. After they got free, and they let 'em come to Texas, they didn't know anything about the 19th of June. In other words, they were free in February, but they didn't find out about this until the 19th of June. On the 19th of June, the first thing they would do is gather all the families that were on the wagon train. You heard me talk about the Hellers, you heard me talk about the Meyenburgs? Those people owned farms, Matt Rile and all. Mama can remember these things. She said Frank and Matt Rile had a farm and those Negroes was on those farms and see after February, well when they made it to Texas, around February. It was somewhere in June, close to June, and then what happened was that, let me tell you what president encouraged them to start the celebration, I can't remember which one, but it was a president that started encouraging the Negroes to have the 19th of June. Because when they had the 19th of June, that meant they sold cases and cases of soda water. Red soda water! Write that down, that was red soda water, they sold cases and cases of red soda water. In Houston, there was a plantation down there, people farmed all down there, Hempstead and Navasota. For the 19th of June, the people always have watermelons ready. They had fresh corn ready, Russian ear corn. This is the way you celebrate, you fried fish, you had bar-b-que and other things.

Reverend Sanders, on the right, was a Baptist preacher. The women loved the preachers; they would cook them dinners regularly.

A young Margaret Martin, Rick Hyman's great-aunt. The window visible in the background would slide horizontally instead of up and down.

Women of the day appear at a local church celebration in the 1920s.

Life on the Henderson Ranch

Mamie: Our relatives organized the Morris Brown AME Church, the Martins, Robersons, and Dobbins. St. Paul was made out of cedar trees, bowed together to make a church. Facing the front door, there is a cemetery on both sides. It's like going into the town of La Grange. They called that area Ann Arbor. This is where they got the lumber to build the church.

To build this church, they sold cotton and lumber. It cost $249 to build it in the 1800s. Mamie's great grandfather, Poleon Roberson, was one of the founders of this church. The Negroes had not graduated to worship in a brick church just yet.

They joined the cedar trees like a tent; then they joined the cedar beams in the center and had a log on both sides. Grandma told me this. Vestar Roberson, they were all along there with Mama's people. Henderson and Lizzie Martin and their daughters belonged to Spring Hill Church in Warrenton. During this time, nobody had no cars, only wagons, buggies, and surreys. They would stay in church all day. In the morning they carried their dinner to church in the wagons. They would sit down on the ground and eat outside the church. They would spread their food outside on the ground so they would not mess up the church. We had some good church.

They would draw the water from the well outside. It had a box around it and a square top with two doors that opened outward to keep rabbits out. It had a lock on it so that nobody could go into the well and put anything harmful in it.

Lullaby Martin, Rick Hyman's great-aunt, eloped with Mr. Chatham, a man from Houston.

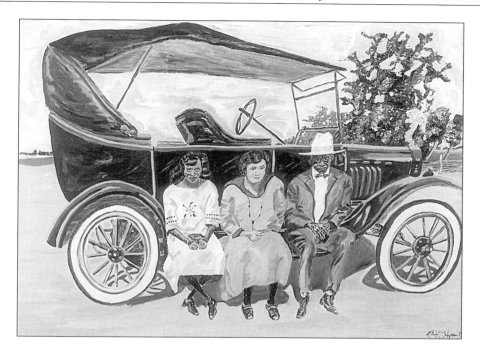

On Daddy's Ranch. *(Acrylic on canvas, 36 in. x 48 in.) Please see p. 119 for the color representation of this painting.*

Aunt Martin (left), Margaret (Tiny) Martin Jones (center), and Elvin Jones (Uncle Monk) sit on one of Henderson Martin's Model T Fords on the Martin ranch in Warrenton (Round Top), Texas, c. 1925.

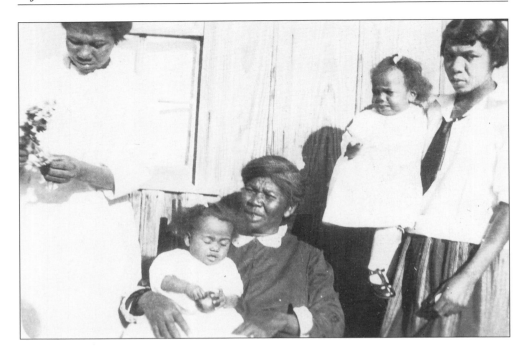

Lizzie Martin (Henderson Martin's wife) and her daughters Margaret and Ethel Mae, with granddaughters Ida Mae Johnson Hyman and Gussie Lee Johnson.

Bernice McLaughlin (left) and a friend play in Henderson Martin's yard.

Katie (left) and Gussie Lee Martin (right).

Elvin Jones (Uncle Monk) helps his father-in-law, Henderson Martin, work on his Model T Ford in 1925. Henderson's crops stretch far in the distance behind Elvin's right shoulder.

My mama would cook food Saturday for church on Sunday. They would put food in a bucket and put it in the well and it would not spoil and then later they'd put ice in the bucket and put it in the well. They had good church back then. We would stay there all day. The last service would be late in the evening before dark and then they would start back home. That was some good country life, son.

All of my people belonged to Spring Hill Church like the Martins did. My grandmother was Ella Jones. Bernice and I were like sister and brother. Uncle Monk would take us to the field. We would play on a cultivator that plows, but when Uncle Monk saw us, he carried us to the house and gave us a good whipping.

When Mr. Henderson Martin got sick, Aunt Tiny would drive him to La Grange to see Dr. Coach (a white doctor). In La Grange, Dr. Cook would deliver the babies. Dr. Cook was black but looked like he was white. Uncle Monk (Elvin Jones) had a good-looking model car. It was not a Ford. Your Aunt Tiny, who was Margaret Martin Jones, was a nice looking red girl. Aunt Serge was a snazzy dresser. Lorene Johnson played basketball. She used to live in La Grange on the Hill by the Colorado River. Then they were more out of the flat to what they call the Hill. They were living the life then! A lot of Negro houses were situated in the Hill. Then they called it the Acre. That's what we called it then. That is somewhere between Elgin and La Grange.

Lullaby Martin met a man named Mr. Chatman out of Houston. Uncle Monk helped this man steal Lullaby away with him to get eloped. Lullaby ran out of the house, and her father, Henderson Martin chased behind them with a shotgun to try to catch them before she escaped. Uncle Monk said that when Lullaby fled the house, she jumped eight strands of barbed wire on her daddy's ranch to get away.

Miss Jessie Lee Hardimon.

An unidentified girl plays with a dog on the farm. The apple boxes and other boxes in the background were used for chickens on the side or back of the barn.

Ellen Martin Johnson holds baby Gussie Lee.

"Lue" is all that was written on the back of this photograph. She is wearing a fur coat and necklace.

Joseph McAlester in Bastrop, Texas.

The Martin family made a good garden. Your Aunt Cornelius, who took the pictures, was the brightest and most educated. She was a teacher and taught at Gravel Hill School. They looked up to her. Aunt Cornelius never got married.

Henderson Martin ruled with an iron hand. Bernice and I would be running through the house, and Henderson Martin would yell, "Sit down!" He could scare a wolf! One time Henderson gave us a dog. The dog got killed on the highway, and I cried and cried. Mr. Henderson Martin said, "Don't cry. You can get another dog." He let me and Aunt Tiny come and get another dog. He was a good man, but he would roar at you, and I was scared of him. Mama's daddy said that all Henderson Martin needed to do was wave his hand and the cattle would lie down and die.

The Martins were kin to the Ligons. The Ligons were good-looking people. William Ligons lived in California. Eliza Ligon and Olivia Ligon are both dead now.

Henderson Martin had a surrey in the 1800s, a two-seater that held four to six people, black with gold fringes. The windows would snap on and off. Not very many black people had this. Henderson Martin had pretty, shiny, dark brown horses that were always well groomed. His horses would trot and then he made them walk single file. I never knew him to ride a horse.

They ate garlic in the morning and evening; it keeps blood pressure down and is good for your heart. They ate onions for potassium. They went out to the woods and got a weed called horse mint. They threw the roots away, boiled the leaves, and sweetened it with honey. They took a few sips for a cold. Henderson sold milk—he put it in galvanized cans. He had to do these things to live.

Henderson Martin dresses a hog. To kill a hog, they would shoot it in the head with a .22 rifle or hit it in the head with an axe. To dress it, Martin would string the pig up on a single tree, cut a slit in each leg, and then put a hook-like object on the pig's leter. Then he would scald the water, shave the pig, and take its insides out.

Country people only bought certain things from the store—flour, salt, sugar, baking powder, and black pepper—the rest they grew themselves. They only went to town on Easter, Christmas, and the 19th of June.

The way women and men got together: they had "suppers" and drank homemade beer (home brewer). If the woman was real nice, you'd have to meet her at church, but if you wanted an uppity woman, you met her at a supper. Henderson met a woman at church.

At first, Henderson Martin did not know he had oil on his land. Back then people used to believe in fortune tellers. They would come by and say that money was buried near the area where Martin lived. They would hit the iron pot, then an object would move, and somebody found money.

There was a man traveling, a man from India who told black people about oil on their land. He got white folks riled up or mad because they did not want black folks to know about oil. He would hit the pot. If you said something, it would move. Some people found money buried under the land.

When Bernice and I were playing at night on the farm, we saw a lot of funny things, then we would get scared and run into the house. We saw strange things like animals appearing and disappearing, pigs and cows and sometimes people. The old folks in the country would say that these were the spirits of dead slaves coming back.

Margaret Martin Jones and her husband, Elvin, on the Martin farm.

We've Come a Long Way

Mamie: Child I pray day and night, I got some scriptures I read so much til I'm almost going blind, son.

Rick: What are some of your favorite scriptures?

Mamie: My favorite scriptures are the 57th psalm, 27th, and 91st. You read that, child, and I tell you I can be so let down and about four o'clock, or two o'clock in the morning, I start reading those psalms, and first thing I know I drift off to sleep.

Rick: We've come a long way, Mamie.

Mamie: You see, the people don't know about this historical legacy of our family. We have to let them know. It is so many people that want to know about black history. You know when I went to school, and that has been a long time ago, if you wanted to find out anything about black people, you had to go to the library. You would not get that in the books, baby.

Rick: Ronda and I were just looking at some of the old photos we have, the ones we showed you, and I am looking at all these black people. I think you told us that they were at Hyde Park with about twenty to thirty automobiles and all of them were blacks out there. I mean, that was really amazing back then in the '20s for blacks to own automobiles, wasn't it?

Ellen Johnson (left) was Rick Hyman's grandmother. She is shown here with her cousin, Lizzie Ligon (right).

My Horse, My Carriage, My Land.
(Acrylic on canvas, 30 in. x 40 in.)
Please see p. 124 for the color
representation of this painting.

George P. Ligon was Lizzie Martin's
father and Rick Hyman's great-great-
grandfather. He is pictured here in
Buckholts, Texas, in September 1921.

George Brown and Etnar Ligon.

Mrs. Kate Smith, a relative of the family, was photographed while visiting the ranch.

Mamie: That's what I'm telling you son. Honey, we have come a long ways. You see, the covered wagons, they did not mind us knowing about that, but when a black man first bought a Model T Ford, then that's when you see, they let them for one day come through La Grange with those Model T Fords. You see, I can remember that. I was a little bitty girl, I must have been about eight or nine years old.

Rick: And you said they let them come through La Grange, Texas?

Mamie: They let them come through from out there in the country. You know everything you had, it could not be in town, it had to be out in the country. Those people had their day. I don't know if it was the 19th of June or what, but it was some celebration they had at Round Top. After they left Round Top, they let them come into La Grange. But don't you think the Highway Patrol and all that, my uncle said, was on the highway behind them like the people were stealing something.

Rick: Uncle Monk told you this, Elvin Jones?

Mamie: That's right. Uncle Monk told me that. But I remember when they got to town because we lived in town. My stepdaddy said, 'child, it is a big day going on.'

Rick: You saw it?

Mamie: I saw the Model T Fords. A bunch of them. There must have been about nine of them. They come on downtown, and they went around the square, and they went out in the country to Arthur Dobbins place. They went out there, they sho' did. Over the bluff.

Rick: So they came through La Grange, and went out there into the country?

Mamie: Yes, they went out there into the country, you know they had to go out into the country quick because those policemen would have started to arrest them. They would have arrested those Negroes, you know that.

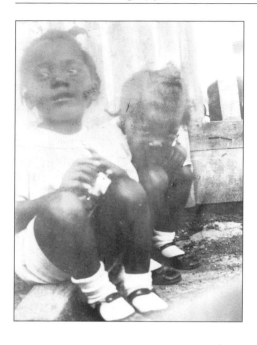

Ida Mae (right) and Gussie Lee (left) Johnson play on the farm.

Mrs. Katie Smith, Ida Mae, and Gussie Lee Johnson.

Gussie Lee Johnson holding Dewitt Martin (Rick Hyman's cousin).

Evelyine Goose holds baby Ida Mae.

At home in their yard in La Grange, Ell and Ellen Johnson play with their daughters, Ida Mae and Gussie Lee.

Ida Mae and Gussie Lee Martin at their home in La Grange.

Rick: And these were black people driving the cars?

Mamie: Them was black people driving them Model T Fords. Everybody had a Model T Ford. My uncle had a little bitty old roadster one, just for him to ride in the front. Others had the two seats, you know, with the curtains you could unbutton.

Rick: Now was Henderson Martin driving his, or was it some other blacks at this time?

Mamie: You know your great grandpa did not drive. His daughter drove, Aunt Tiny.

Rick: But they were in that parade?

Mamie: Honey, he was setting in there, honey. Sure was, Aunt Tiny was the one driving, Uncle Monk's wife, but then there were them other sisters and Mr. Henderson Martin, he was in there too. But you know, Mr. Martin, he never drove, he had two sons that drove, Guy Martin and Connie Lee Martin. They drove for him before Aunt Tiny came on the scene. I ain't ever going to forget that.

Rick: You saw him and the rest of them coming through there?

Mamie: I saw him in that Ford, child, coming through La Grange. Cause my stepdaddy had bought one. But that was going on, baby!

Rick: All of the black folks were proud to see that, weren't they?

Mamie: You know they were proud to see that. That was a celebration, what you talking about.

Minnie Lomas and Janetta at Spring Hill College. This location was the scene of the black-and-white photo, and later, the painting, of the 1921 women's basketball team. The painting is entitled Undefeated.

Rick: Were a lot of people out watching this?

Mamie: Sure they was out there. Even the white folks come out to look at those Negroes come through there, child. The police and the Highway Patrol with them old white cars with the black thing on it, honey they went from out to Round Top and all the way to La Grange following them Negroes.

Rick: So they were helping them make it through?

Mamie: I guess they was, or they wanted to arrest them one. I can't say what it was, but when they went around that square in town there was Mr. Will Loessin, he was the big wheel in town then. Mr. Will Loessin from out there in the country.

Rick: Was he white?

Mamie: Yeah, he was white. He had a habit for stopping all the black folks that were driving their cars into town. Then there was Mr. Dipple, old Mr. Dipple. Mr. Jim Flinall (a white man) was a Texas Ranger before he came to La Grange as the High Sheriff. He was real tall and handsome, slim and no belly. He wore a Stetson hat. His hair was dark black and he did not wear a mustache. He was one of the first ones in town to have a Model A Ford. Mr. Flinall ran Mr. Dipple out of town. That's right, he was the big wheel, baby. He had been with the Texas Rangers and he knew what was going on. Anytime a Negro came to La Grange driving in an automobile after that parade, they would arrest them. If they come up there in a good-looking car, they would arrest them, until Mr. Jim Flinall came on the scene. When he came on the scene he stopped that mess. He told them that everybody was equal to something.

Ellen Johnson, Ida Mae Johnson Hyman, and Gussie Lee Johnson are pictured with their dog.

Ida Mae, Gussie Lee, and relative Katie (middle).

C.E. Smith is pictured in the center of this snowy scene in Texas.

Etnar Ligon, Ellen Martin's cousin.

People gather outside for a Sunday church event.

Rick: Now around what year was this, when you saw the parade and all?

Mamie: Oh God, I can't remember all that cause I was just about nine years old honey. I was born in 1925.

Rick: Did they only have that parade in town one year?

Mamie: They only did that one year, and never did that no more. Then they started letting them go up there to the fairground, after that, to keep them out of town. They had to come through the country, and when you come through the country you automatically come through the fairground. They did not allow them to come to town no more like that, you hear?

Rick: So they had already planned this celebration that they were going to drive through the town?

Mamie: Those Negroes had already planned it when they drove from the church in Round Top. I don't know who the pastor was then cause I was too young to remember. Mama sho' don't know either. And ain't nobody around to tell us cause you know all the old people is dead that moved from out there. But anyway, I know that it was a preacher out there in Round Top. I do know that he was the instigator of all this going to town stuff.

Rick: Where was Mr. Martin riding most of the time when people were driving him around in his Model T Ford? The back seat or the front?

Mamie: Now you know he sat in the back! Because his girls were in the front. But one was sat beside him in the back, you know one was driving and the other was sitting back there.

Rick: Did he have his hat on?

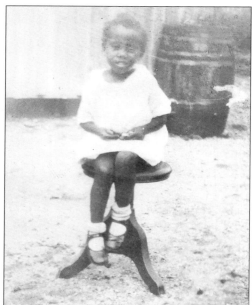

Gussie C. Martin, Rick Hyman's great aunt, at the Martin's home.

Gussie C. Martin as a child.

Mamie: You know he had to have that hat on, he could not make it without it. He wore that hat at all times. Him and another man called Mr. Ellison Ferguson, they wore them Stetsons, honey. He did not wear nothing else. Pops always had to have a good hat. He'd make them take him to La Grange to get his hat, baby. My uncle would say, "Let me take this old man over here and get him another hat."

Rick: Well, Stetson is the top of the line. Did he buy a lot of hats?

Mamie: He had a black one and a white-looking one. Sure was, that black one was for funerals. Well you know it was a tradition. People back then had traditions, they don't have traditions now. Certain things, if it was a funeral you did not have to be kin to that person, but you wore black. That's right, you went to the funeral and you knew how to dress. You had certain things to wear.

Rick: Who did they buy the cars from? I mean, being black, would they let the blacks buy cars?

Mamie: Yeah, if they had the money! It was a man, I forget what his name was, if it comes to me I'll let you know. I'll tell you who it was; Milton Teaman was the instigator of that celebration in La Grange. Auto Rank was the one that had them cars for sale. That's right, he was the one that sold them Ford cars.

Rick: Was he a white man?

Mamie: You know he was a white man. What do you think? Them Negroes were out there on Hellers farm and they were making that money, you know they could get a car. What's wrong with you?

From left to right are Isaac Moore, Roberta Rivers, and C.W. Dickson.

Evelyn (left) and Serge Martin, Henderson's daughter (right). Serge was the mother of Bernice McLaughlin, Rick Hyman's second cousin.

Artri Dobbins was the husband of Rick Hyman's great-aunt Ethel Mae Martin Dobbins. Rick Hyman had the pleasure of meeting his great-uncle in Houston.

From left to right are Ida Mae Johnson Hyman, Bernice McLaughlin, and Gussie Lee Johnson.

Rick: So they just went in and bought a car? What town was Auto Rank located in?
Mamie: Right there in Warrenton, Texas. Little old place Warrenton. They had a gin and a couple of stores there. One man across the street was named Mr. Jesse Teaman. Mack Zapp was the big store. Mr. Jesse Teaman, he owned the mill and cotton gin.
Rick: Would you say that Henderson Martin was one of the first ones to buy a Model T Ford? For black folks in this part of Texas?
Mamie: I would say he was. I don't know anybody else who got it before he did. Cause he was the Big Wheel. Everybody at church would say, "yonder goes Henderson Martin!" That's what they called him cause he stood out. The others started following suit. I think Boyd Jones and them, no kin to Mama, he was another one that got that car. He worked and was in Rutersville, but he had to come over to Auto Rank to get the car. They lived out in Rutersville on a farm.
Rick: Tell me about the 19th of June.
Mamie: When I remember the 19th of June, I remember that they would have two wash pots, they would cut up fish and fry them. Somebody would make ten pounds of Irish potatoes after they were peeled and cooked. They would have Irish potato salad, cakes, pies, and honey, they had lemonade, and they would use this color.

You heard your mother talk about cake color, well, they would put that coloring in the lemonade. You could have red, pink, or green lemonade, and they would put them in those great big old crock pots, set up on the floor.

Rick: Now was this around the time when you were a little girl?

Mamie: Yes sir, when I was a little girl, and on after I got grown. When I got grown, they started to barbecuing, and did not fry the fish like they did a long time ago. They would stay up all night barbecuing ribs and what have you. And they would come into La Grange, and get all of that La Grange sausage and things, throw them on the pit and let them get hot. Ooh, it was good, child. Fried them chickens and things, they would have fried chickens, barbecue chickens, baked chickens. So honey, you see, we got rich then, we did not have to have that other stuff. Ooh, but they would be some good old times. They had the 19th of June out there at Arthur Dobbins's place. One celebration would be there. Out from Round Top, it was a park up there. Some would be there, over in the night they would be at Collins Park, they'd have it out there and then the big deal would be going back over to Arthur Dobbins. They'd have a dance out there at night. Oh yes, child, that was when I was old enough to know what was going on. I must have been about 15 or 16 years old (1940).

Rick: Were the Dobbins kin to us?

Mamie: Oh yes.

Rick: Did they come over on the wagon train?

Mamie: Sure they had to come over here, everybody had to come over here from slavery. It wasn't no people here in Texas that wasn't slaves. Everybody come over here, they just came with different people. See that's how that fella Heller bought a lot of them people, that's how it was Heller's farm. Then it was another farm, they called it Will Loessin's farm. Then they had A.V. Smith's farm. All them Negroes were on a farm honey.

Rick: So they were working on these farms at the time. Were they like plantations?

Mamie: Honey, it was a plantation or something. Everybody was farming.

Rick: Even though it was not slavery?

Mamie: It was not slavery. Let me tell you what it was called. In December, people had finished picking cotton and everything, and they had what they called a Land Law. The owner of the farm would advance them people who stayed on the farm until March. And see, in March, most farmers had their potatoes, Irish potatoes, and all that stuff. They had English peas, collard greens, cabbage, and the corn would have multiplied, son.

Rick: So it was like sharecropping?

Mamie: That's what it was called. All right, now let me tell you about the first Negro back out that way going towards Warrenton and Round Top where your great-grandpa, Henderson Martin, lived. He used to sharecrop and the first time he made a good crop sharing with them people, he put away some money on a home. Henderson Martin did not sharecrop a long time like the rest of them did. No sir. Henderson Martin had his farm up there. My Uncle Monk was working for some more people 'cause he married Martin's daughter. I'm telling you, Henderson stood

A studio shot of Mabel Ligon, c. 1925. Notice the intricate carvings on the chair in which she sits. Buttons leading to the knees like the ones on her dress must have been the style at that time.

on his feet. I tell you they say, "yonder goes old man Henderson Martin. Yonder goes old Martin." They would say that whenever he passed by, cause he was up there. You know how Negroes were. That made them kind of envious. He was nice and neat.

Rick: He bought his first farm before he was married, didn't he?

Mamie: I'm telling you, he did. When he got married in October 1891, he took mama (his wife) on home to their house. It wasn't no big house like it is now; it was what they call one of them shotgun houses, as my uncle would say. Then he added on and added on as the children come along, until he had a nice home and then he remodeled it.

Rick: Tell me about how Morris and Brown were two separate people who gave the church its name.

Mamie: It was two separate people, Morris Brown. One man's name was orris, they called him Morris, but see, he was a Roberson, our kinfolk. His name was Morris Roberson, but everybody called him Bead. You heard of Bead Roberson?

Rick: Yes.

Mamie: That was who that was, Morris Roberson. And then Mr. Brown was Lucindy Brown's husband. So that is how the church got its name.

Rick: How did they get the money to build the church?

Mamie: They sold lumber and cotton and everybody worked together to get a loan. Mr. Brown stood for the loan. Him and my great uncle (Roberson) co-signed. They went to Matt Rile to get the loan. That was up in Walhalla, but the loan came from Warrenton.

Rick: Once they got the loan, did they start to build the church?

Mamie: They built that church, first they had the school in the church. Then in later years, the white people donated a piece of ground not far from Matt Rile's store. Right behind the store they donated a piece of ground for a school for the black children, of course. Because it was so many children that lived on Hellers farm, they had to build a little school. They called it Walhalla School.

Rick: I guess when they first settled they were on Hellers farm. How many Negroes do you think were living on there at one time?

Mamie: Oh, I guess it must have been about nine families, maybe more than that. There was the Kimble family, the Brown family. Everybody called this man Cut, but he was a Roberson. He was there, and then there was Mr. Brown. There were three sets of Browns out there.

Rick: Now, our people were out there too, right?

Mamie: They sure were, honey, the Robersons and the Martins. Bead Roberson was the offspring of Poleon Roberson; Poleon was Bead's daddy. Their mama's name was Lizzie Roberson. The Robersons took the slave master's name from Virginia.

Rick: Was Roberson a good slave master or a bad one?

Mamie: You know those house Negroes had good deals, but when they were in the fields they had to, you know, bring it on up there. This is what my great-granddaddy told me.

Aunt Serge Martin (third from the far right), Ethel Mae Martin (second from the left) and Evelyn are pictured wearing their jewelry with three other unidentified women.

A proud relative poses on the Martin Ranch with a chicken pen in the background.

In this photo, J.L. is in the middle. Model T Fords appear in the background.

Rick: This is what Poleon Roberson told you?

Mamie: Poleon Roberson and Great-grandma Lizzie said that those house Negroes had it good. But those that worked in the field, they did not have it too good, cause they went from sun up to sun down. But that's history, baby. And you know what? We suppose to have freedom now, but we don't have too much freedom as it is, in some instances.

Rick: Yes, but you know these pictures show that they have come a long way.

Mamie: Oh my God! That's almost like day from night.

Rick: It's incredible, a family coming from on a wagon train from slavery just making it in the wilderness.

Mamie: The bears and animals did not mess with them people. How do you think they made it through those terrible thickets and woods?

Rick: I guess Poleon was praying all along the way?

Mamie: That's right, because he was a preacher, you know. That Grandma Lizzie, she was the mother of 13 kids. I can hear mama's mama say that her mother said it was about nine wagons altogether that came through the country from Virginia. Them people all came to Texas in covered wagons. By the time they arrived, there was only 120 of them.

Rick: Did she say how big a plantation she came from?

Mamie: No, they didn't. It was not too many people who could read or write at that time; that was kind of rare for those people then. Just a few of those people that worked in the house could. These were the house slaves that learned how to read and write. In fact, my great-grandma said that if they caught them reading they got a real good beating. Lizzie Roberson, Poleon Roberson's wife, told that to grandma and them, and grandma handed it down to us. That's how that come on down, from generation to generation.

Mamie: They were there, and they knew what was going on. If they got caught reading, they would get a terrible beating. She said that if some of them house Negroes were in the kitchen and they be done cooking, they would get the grease and rub them people down where they would have beat them so.

Rick: To kind of heal them, to ease the pain?

Mamie: Yes, now you know that was horrible!

Rick: Yes. Yes, it was.

End of visit with Mamie: Cousin Mamie said that Henderson Martin was well respected, but she was afraid of him. She said he was good for the community. Sometimes some of the young men in the area would sneak on Henderson's farm and go under a tree. Henderson would sit down with them and talk and counsel them, and explain things and keep them out of trouble. Mamie, her 98-year-old mother, and her daughter, with me in the middle, held hands and prayed before I left to return to Virginia. I knelt between the two women who went back almost a hundred years and prayed to God to bless us and our ancestors.

C.E. Smith.

Ell and Ellen Johnson with their baby, Ida Mae.

Ruby Louise Poole holds baby Ida Mae Johnson.

Conversations with Cousin Bernice:
Remembrances of Henderson Martin

Henderson Martin worked all summer. School was over about the middle of April so the kids could go to the field. It started again about the middle of September. In the 1870s, Henderson Martin was a young man, and he worked for an old white man named Martin Liggons. He looked like Santa Claus with his long white hair and long white beard, he wore bib overalls. Liggons's parents had money—that's how it was back then. When a family had money, they hired a black person to work for them and raise their children and a black woman worked in the kitchen. This was Martin Liggons's family. Grandpa worked for him, and he paid Grandpa 40¢ on the dollar. Grandpa chopped cotton for him from sun up to sun down. They would give you one meal, the noon meal. That's why the average black person was willing to take 40 acres and a mule. But Grandpa wanted more than that. Henderson Martin's sister, Vicey Martin Dotson, had four thousand acres of land in Giddings, Texas. Giddings is oil and cattle country.

Henderson Martin bought himself a used wooden double bed. He brought it home with no springs on it because he did not want to sleep on the floor anymore. His mother took the bed away from him and gave it to his oldest sister, who was twelve years old when she got married. She married a white man and had a whole lot of children. He took her to California where they could live and she did not have to hide or be ashamed of her half-white children, where he could own her.

Lizzie Martin (left) and Cornelius Martin (right). Lizzie was Henderson Martin's wife, and Cornelius was their daughter. She was the only one of his children that he let drive his car. Henderson and Lizzie knew they could depend on her. She was a schoolteacher and very smart. She attended Prairie View College in Texas.

Henderson Martin, An American Legend. *(Acrylic on canvas, 40 in. x 30 in.) Please see p. 121 for a color representation of this painting. Inset: Henderson Martin poses with one of his Fords on his farm in 1925. Henderson (Rick Hyman's great-grandfather) was a cattle rancher who owned over 2,000 acres of oil land in Texas, as well as four Model T and Model A Fords, a stagecoach, carriage, and an abundance of silver and jewelry.*

Gussie Lee Johnson (back, left), Ida Mae Johnson (back, right), Bernice McLaughlin (front, left), and Willie Martin (front, right).

Grandpa said he cried and cried when they took his bed away, but it did not mean anything. He said he wanted to go to school, so Mr. Liggons fixed him a room onto his house. He had chores after school. He went to school until the seventh grade and then he quit at about age 16. It was an all-black school.

Martin Liggons was from New York. They came to Texas for one thing, to buy land. He bought five thousand acres.

We have some cousins in La Grange, Margarite Ligon Plummer. The oldest one is 90. The Ligons (black) were good time people; they had buggies with rubber tires. The Ligons (Henderson's wife's family) did not have land, but they had real nice horses. There is no blood relation between the black Ligons and the white Liggons.

Old man Ligon did not carry his family in a wagon like Grandpa Martin did. He carried his family in a hat. All of Grandma Martin's family died from tuberculosis. Her nieces and nephew lived on the Colorado River. They did not believe in school. But old man Liggons (white man) made Henderson Martin go to school. He rode a mule to school in Walhalla.

In the old days, in Grandpa's day, you had to have a thousand acres before you could call it a ranch. The place he bought was 70 acres. The land that Grandpa inherited from Martin Liggons was about two thousand acres. I don't know how much more. It was in Fayette County between Warrenton and Round Top.

Grandpa never had a decent team of mules; he raised a nice herd of beautiful cattle. He died February 16, 1935, when I was about seven years old. I remember that he wore a silver belly hat (white cowboy hat) and cowboy boots up to his knees. He was always a cowboy. You'd never see him with overalls on. He always carried a shotgun.

Connie Lee Martin and Gussie Martin taught class in this one-room schoolhouse. They were Rick Hyman's great-aunt and -uncle. All of the members of the Martin family stressed the importance of education among their children.

Bessie Martin (left) and Sadie Paige Martin (right standing), mother of Eliza Martin Calhoun, who now resides in California.

Neighbor kids pose in front of a tree in Henderson Martin's yard.

Bernice McLaughlin (left) appears with Connie Lee Martin's children, Massie (middle girl) and Vastine (far right boy).

A church affair at Robinson or Plum, Texas. The Martins and Ligons are in this photo.

Henderson Martin, Rick Hyman's great-grandfather..

Gussie C. Martin, Rick Hyman's great-aunt.

95

CONVERSATIONS WITH UNCLE WILLIE:
"We Earned Our Livin'!"

This conversation took place between Rick Hyman and Uncle Willie during a visit to Willie's Texas home in May 1997.

Willie: Guy Martin was my daddy. Henderson Martin (my grandfather) lived between Warrenton and Round Top. I was born in 1928. Your mother, Ida Mae, is older than me, and I'm older than my brother, Raymond. Back in my time, it was just like slavery time. The first job I had, I was 13 years old. My daddy hired me to chop cotton for a man. I had to walk three miles to work and I got paid 49¢ a day. I did not get nare penny. But I was happy. I had to take care of my little sisters and brothers.

Rick: Around what year was that when you were picking cotton?

Willie: About 1939.

Rick: What part of Texas was that?

Willie: Up there in La Grange, Fayette County area. They used to say, old man Henderson Martin, they said those white people did not mess with him because they said he was crazy. I imagine he was crazy if you mess with him. You'd have to kill him. A white man is a funny thing. If he sees you have a bunch of little hungry children, and you're trying to make it, God will move on him to say, 'don't mess with that poor Negro, he's trying to raise a family, he's trying to make it.' Any man knows the difference in right from wrong.

Rick: Henderson Martin was something for his day, wasn't he?

Willie: I remember when I was a little boy and me, Bernice, Raymond, and old Grandpa (Henderson Martin) we used to leave from down there in Warrenton and Round Top and go to La Grange with him sometime. He had an old white horse hooked to the buckboard wagon and he would put that old 30-30 rifle somewhere under that buggy, and he had a piece of bullet about the size of your big finger. He would say, "it would shoot today and kill tomorrow." It [the bullet] liked to go two miles, when you shoot it. They would meet another white person's buggy up and down the road and they would stop and talk to one another. White folks knew how far to go with him.

Rick: I heard he went in town one time and got ambushed and had to shoot his way out.

Willie: Yes, he did. My aunt told me about it, Aunt Bessie, my daddy's oldest sister.

Rick: What did she say?

Willie: That they hemmed him up and he had to let them know that he was not scared.

Women in the Field. *(Acrylic on canvas, 36 in. x 48 in.) Please see p. 120 for a color representation of this painting.*

Lizzie Martin (center), Henderson Martin's wife, with a sack of already-picked cotton to the left.

Rick: Did he kill that man he shot?

Willie: I don't know. I was too young to know.

Willie: Aunt Bessie knew how to provide for a family. I grew up knowing hard work. I started pickin cotton when I was five years old.

Rick: Was it pretty tough picking cotton?

Willie: Yeah, it was tough, especially when you got a butt-cuttin' to go along with it. I was five years old and I remember one Saturday evening, I was tired. I was pickin cotton and it was around sundown. Man, I was tired! At the time, I was little and I was resting my arms, my elbows on my knees. My Dad looked back and saw that. And my daddy pulled up a stalk of cotton with boles, hulles, and all and shot that on my back end. You talk about a little colored boy pickin' cotton, I went on and got that cotton! Thing about a whippin', you gotta start on a child when he is little, cause if you don't give him a whippin', you're about to get whipped.

Lullaby Martin, Rick Hyman's great-aunt, on the Martin ranch.

Joel Robinson and his car at Hyde Park..

E. Bell and Rick Hyman's grandfather, Ell Johnson (second from left), at a shipping company or depot in Houston.

Thoughts in Closing

by Rick Hyman

My great grandfather, Henderson Martin, was a leader and stood up for freedom and equal rights for himself and all people. The chapters tell of two incidents of this. The first one took place around the 1880s with his gun battle in town, and the second one with him riding in his car in a caravan of eight other Model T Fords, all owned and driven by African Americans around the square downtown. I feel this was their way of a non-violent protest for equality along with just celebrating a great event at church. My great-grandfather and the others in those automobiles knew that blacks were not supposed to be driving their cars in town and they came very close to getting arrested or lynched. But, as Cousin Mamie said, "This was a great day!" Not long after this occurred, blacks were finally allowed to drive their cars in town, due to a former Texas Ranger who became the new high sheriff and changed things. I thank God for these changes, and for my Texas family!

Ethel Martin is pictured on the far right.

Connie Lee Martin, Rick Hyman's great-uncle.

Reverend and Ruby Medlock.

This Hyman relative was a schoolteacher at Hyde Park in East Chapel, Texas. She poses here with her automobile, tag number 896-450 TX.

Lizzie Martin, Ethel Mae Martin, and little Ida Mae Johnson Hyman.

Chapter Three

HENDERSON MARTIN'S DESCENDANTS

(1940–2000)

Gussie Lee Martin Johnson (left) and her sister, Ida Mae Johnson Hyman (right), in the 1940s. Both of them attended Wiley College in Marshall, Texas, in the 1940s. Aunt Gussie continued to preserve the family photos, and at her death in 1981, passed them on to her sister Ida Mae, Rick Hyman's mother.

Rick Hyman's parents, Ida Mae Johnson Hyman and Bruce Leo Hyman Sr., at their home in Washington, D.C. in 1951. The author's parents met in church and then two weeks later, they got married. They were married for 22 years until his death in 1975. They had a wonderful marriage and both were active at church and in the community during their lifetime together.

Rick Hyman's grandparents, Ell Shropshire Johnson and Ellen Martin Johnson, posed for this portrait in Houston. They were both from La Grange, Texas. They lived in Houston's Third Ward on Delano Street.

Great-uncle Willie Martin on his front porch in Egypt, Texas. Hyman painted a picture of Willie in the painting Yesteryear. *See the color representation on p. 123. Willie spent time on the Henderson Martin ranch as a youth.*

Great-uncle Raymond Martin on his farm in Egypt, Texas. Rick Hyman sees a strong resemblance between Uncle Raymond and Henderson Martin.

From left to right are Cynthia Martin (Raymond Martin's daughter-in-law), Raymond Martin (Henderson Martin's grandson), and Marjorie Martin Tones (Raymond Martin's daughter).

Ida Mae Johnson Hyman (Rick Hyman's mother) poses with cousins Evelyn McLaughlin (far left), her husband Benice McLaughlin (middle), and their daughter Veronica McLaughlin at the Astrodome in Houston, Texas, during a rodeo in 1985.

Rick Hyman, shown here at the age of five (left) and on his way to a rodeo on February 20, 1985 (right), learned to love the Old West and Texas at an early age. He liked to watch Westerns. His favorite cowboys were Randolph Scott, Roy Rogers, and John Wayne. He even met the Lone Ranger once on the grounds of the Washington Monument.

Rick Hyman and his youngest daughter, Ellen Merissa Hyman, took this picture together in Austin, Texas, in 1995.

Rick Hyman with two of his daughters, Brianna Hardison (left) and Christy Hardison Bean (right), at the Hyman's home in Virginia, in 1997.

In 1997, cousin Mamie Paige White posed with Rick Hyman's wife, Ronda Cain Hyman, under a tree in Mamie's front yard in Houston. Mamie is like a mother to Rick and Ronda Hyman. She talked with Rick and Ronda numerous times about their family history.

Eliza Martin Calhoun (lower center) and her husband, Everett Calhoun (lower left), pose with their children, Everett Calhoun Jr., Yolonda Calhoun (top center), Veronda Proctor (top right), and Theresa Hiter (top left). The family now resides in California, except for Veronda, who lives in Georgia with her husband.

Ryan Jones, the son of R.B. Tones and Marjorie Tones. He lives in Houston.

Raymond Jellon Martin III. He is the son of Raymond Marti Jr.

Chapter Four

THE HYMAN
COLLECTION OF JEWELRY

This jewelry was worn by African Americans at the turn of the 20th century. Most likely, it was bought by the family in La Grange, at Hermes and Meyenburg's jewelry store. Mamie Paige White (Henderson Martin's granddaughter) bought her watches at Meyenburg's. Some of the jewelry may have been purchased in Round Top. During slavery, white masters would give the "house niggers" jewelry for their birthdays and other holidays. It was passed down from generation to generation, and finally discovered hidden away in the same dresser drawer as the family photos. Many of the pieces can be seen on family members in the black and white photographs. All pieces featured in this book have been appraised and are now part of the Hyman Collection.

Opposite Above: (top left) goldplated bracelet (1880s–1910s); (top center and bottom center) jewelry set consisting of a necklace and bracelet (1880s–1890s); (left, second from top) bracelet consisting of eight simulated stones in silvertone mounts (1930s–1970s); (left, third from top) bracelet (1930s-1960s); (left, bottom) bracelet with bars of silvertone and black- and turquoise-colored plastic (1940s–1950s); (right, second from top) bracelet with carved bone rosettes and molded plastic Oriental faces in silvertone mounts 1920s–1930s); (right, second from bottom) bracelet of six ovals of brown/white slag glass with plastic flecks, leafy sides, and a lion or dog head on top (1930s–1950s).

Opposite Below: (clockwise from top left to right) crescent-shaped goldtone brooch (1910s); bee-shaped goldtone brooch with wings on springs (1950s); earrings of red glass made to look like garnets (1920s-1930s); red glass brooch with goldtone mounts (1920s-1930s); red glass bracelet with goldtone mounts (1930s-1940s); goldplated double-chain bracelet (1920s-1930s); necklace of green glass with goldtone loops (1890s-1920s); quasi-triangular brooch with three round lobes with centered robin's egg blue glass stone and three ovals, surrounded by three crescents of round blue stones, punctuated by three large and three small seed pearls, in beaded scalloped outside frame (1920s-1930s); brooch stamped "SANDOR," consisting of four pearls, each drilled, set with prongs into goldtone mounts within two mother-of-pearl leaves and tendril (1920s-1930s); silvertone bracelet (1930s-1950s).

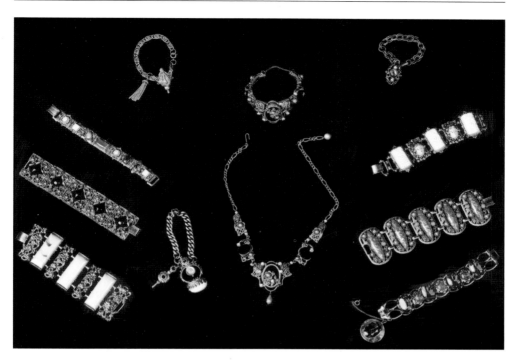

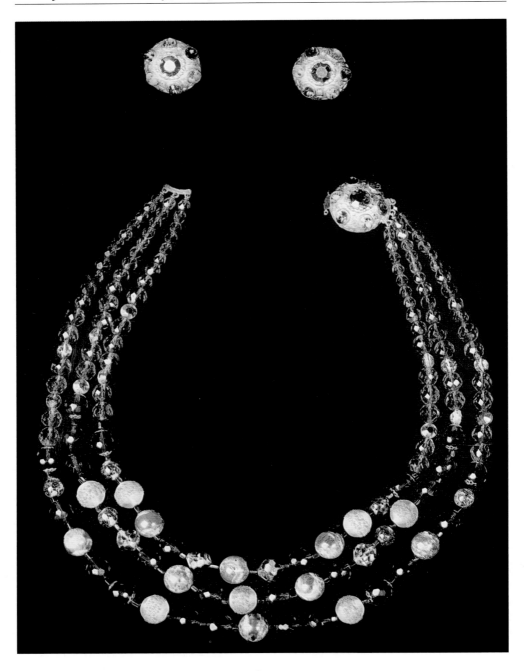

The 1920s clip-on earrings at the top each have a domed shape hemisphere in the same design as the clasp of the necklace below. This necklace consists of three strands of graduated faceted green glass beads plus round quartz and round glass beads with green dots on the surface and a round domed goldtone clasp. Overall it is 26". This piece is also from the 1920s, although the clasp may date later than the beads.

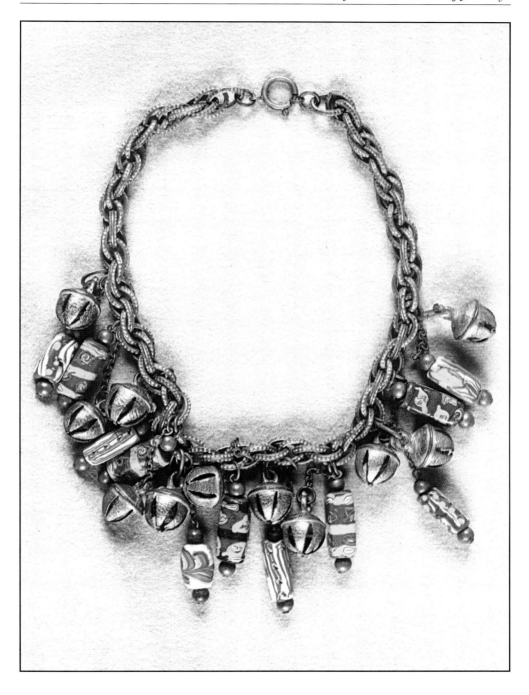

This necklace consists of brass loops plus eleven goldtone brass bells plus eleven African glass bar beads, each a quadrate bar of multicolors. These beads are known as trade beads, originating in Murano, Italy (1900-1930s).

Chapter Five

RICK HYMAN'S
HISTORICAL PAINTINGS

My Texas Family. *(Acrylic on canvas, 30 in. x 40 in.) "I decided to paint this picture after showing my late uncle, Dr. Mark Hyman, historian and author, the vintage photo of it. He said, 'If you paint this picture with these people sitting on the side of the car you will really have something.' I knew from the beginning that this picture was going to be super special. I say this because I was painting my great-grandparents and their children. I guess you could say that their spirit was with me while I was painting. I wanted to show them standing firm on their land as if they are about to weather a storm approaching from the horizon with the clouds forming. A print of this painting was on the set of Cosby, the television show on CBS. It also won an award for painting in the first juried show for black artists in the state of Virginia at the Daura Gallery at Lynchburg College in Lynchburg, Virginia."*

Romance Lady. *(Acrylic on canvas, 40 in. x 30 in.) "I envisioned the dress and hat to be a purple color before I painted this picture. I knew that I had to make the rocks sharp and rugged at times. The most important part of this painting is the posture of the female and her hat."*

Above: Undefeated. *(Acrylic on canvas, 36 in. x 48 in.)* "*I feel the most important part of this painting is the spirits you see in their faces and their head wraps. It was very difficult to paint the headwraps. These are some tough-looking basketball players and they look as though they would not let any team beat them, so I named it "Undefeated." The uniforms were painted as though you know these people were once here but are now long gone. So you know you are looking at the past. I painted the brick mortar and stone as though I, myself, was some of this material and I just let it flow. I held my breath every step of the way.*"

Opposite Above: On Daddy's Ranch. *(Acrylic on canvas, 36 in. x 48 in.)* "*This painting was one of my late Uncle Dr. Mark Hyman's favorites. I painted the people's faces first, then I painted their hands, their clothes, the car, and then the background. It was a joy to paint scenes like this one, knowing that my great-granddaddy had thousands of acres of land, that all the land you see in the picture, all the way to the horizons and hills, is his property.*"

Opposite Below: Southern Gentlemen on a Sunday Afternoon. *(Acrylic on canvas, 30 in. x 40 in.)* "*Every picture I paint, I see more detail. This is the first time I painted a newspaper. The man to the far right is reading a newspaper. I guess he is letting the world know that we are intelligent enough to read. I painted pocket watches and the Stetson hats. The wooden buildings in the background shows that it is a rural setting.*"

Women in the Field. *(Acrylic on canvas, 36 in. x 48 in.) "There is something about the way these women are positioned and their look and their dress that fascinated me and I just knew I had to paint this one. The looks on their faces especially the lady on the far right intrigued me, and also their hats. All of them are standing proudly in the field. I closely looked at the black-and-white photo I painted this from in an attempt to see what the white object to the far left was. I did not know if it was sheep, or a bail of cotton. I decided to leave it out. I have been told by a relative that it is probably a sack of picked cotton."*

Henderson Martin, An American Legend. *(Acrylic on canvas, 40 in. x 30 in.) "When I decided that it was time to paint this picture after studying it for almost three years, I came to the conclusion that the most important part was his profile and the Silver Belly, or as we call them today, his Stetson hat. I decided that nothing in the picture would conflict or distract the viewer from Mr. Martin and his hat, especially no other colors the same tone of his hat. The light color of faint blue clouds to the right I painted to show that Henderson Martin can faintly see a glimpse of the future for his family and it shines through as though the ancestors are saying, 'Yes, the future will get better, there is a glimmer of hope.' So in this painting I would have to say that Mr. Martin is looking at his past, reminiscing and feeling close to God, and the light clouds show him wondering what the future holds for his people and for all people."*

Making Our Way to Something Better. *(Acrylic on canvas, 7 ft. x 8 ft.) This painting is based on oral family history as it was told to Rick Hyman by his cousin, Mamie Paige White, of Houston, Texas. In striking colors and detail, it depicts Hyman's ancestors (the Martins, Ligons, and Robersons), just freed from slavery, making their way from Virginia to Texas in covered wagons around 1866. This painting, along with eight other Hyman works, was exhibited during the month of February 1998 for Union Station's 90th anniversary in Washington D.C to celebrate Black History Month. The exhibition was sponsored by the National Council of Negro Women. "To the right of the painting, the sky is red, which symbolizes the pain and bloodshed as they left the plantation and slavery. I painted the other clouds as though there is a sky filled with an army of angels watching, protecting and guiding this wagon train of ex-slaves, my ancestors, to a new life."*

A Woman's Spirit. *(Acrylic on canvas, 40 in. x 30 in.)*

Yesteryear. *(Acrylic on canvas, 36 in. x 48 in.)* "I chose the title for this painting after I saw that there is a horse hitched to a buckboard wagon in the background. The horse is turning his head towards the camera as though he is saying to the little boys, 'Hey, don't forget about me, I carried you and your family for over the past 100 years.' Not only am I the artist, but also the great grandson with a strong passion to paint my family from this time period. I am the bloodline and continuity of the family. These photos I have found are rarely seen of middle-class African-American life in the early 1900s. This is American history, not just African-American history."

My Horse, My Carriage, My Land. *(Acrylic on canvas, 30 in. X 40 in.) "It was very important for me to show the strong character and self-esteem of my great-great-grandfather in this painting. My favorite part of this painting is the wagon wheels and the shadow between them. This painting was juried into a show at the Salmagundi Club on Fifth Avenue in New York."*

Love Forever, Sis. *(Acrylic on canvas, 48 in. x 36 in.) "I chose this title for this because of the arms resting on each sister as though they are connected forever. I love the hairstyles and shoes and dresses against a pioneer-type dwelling."*

Hattie Plays Her Mandolin. *(Acrylic on canvas, 36 in. x 30 in.)*

My Three Ancestors. *(Fabric and acrylic on canvas, 55 in. X 65 in.) "After Cousin Mamie told me about my ancestors journey on the covered wagon train to Texas and how they encountered the Native Americans and became friends and even intermarried, I imagined this scene. The two chiefs are in a peaceful posture with the African-American freed slave between them. I did this to show that he is sitting amongst royalty and that he is just as deserving because he has a strong royal heritage also. All three were my ancestors because all of their blood runs through my body along with other bloodlines."*

Parasol in the Park. *(Acrylic on canvas, 40 in.x 30 in.) "I imagined this scene as if it were a French painting. Maybe it is the parasol. I always see the picture finished in my mind or when I am asleep before the actual painting is completed."*

126

From These Beginnings. *(Acrylic on canvas, 10 ft. X 8 ft.) This signature piece was first displayed at Union Station in Washington, D.C., during the month of February 1998. Hyman consults with his wife, Ronda, on each painting in choosing colors and making key decisions. In one of their conversations about his works, Ronda said of the women depicted in his artwork, "I believe that women of all nationalities will immerse themselves in the colors and brushstrokes that create in the women's faces and posture a demeanor that is real and natural, persuasive and engaging."*

Family Tree. *(Acrylic on canvas, 30 in. x 40 in.) "I painted this picture in a desperate attempt to show all eyes were looking at the viewer, but yet not a smile anywhere. If I had used the same colors for the dresses it would be a boring picture. The more I painted, the more detail I noticed, like the buttons on the dresses. There is no silverware on the table. This painting was a challenge because it was one of the first scenes I painted with a large group of people in it. I like painting group portraits. After I painted this I just happened to count the number of people and the number of tree branches and they both came to the number 21."*

"May God and our ancestors in Heaven

smile and say, 'Job well done, for this

family legacy finally being told.' "

—Rick Hyman, 2000